THE COMPLETE IDIOT'S GUIDE® TO

The Chemistry of Love

by Maryanne Fisher, Ph.D.,
with Victoria Costello

ALPHA

A member of Penguin Group (USA) Inc.

To my students to help them keep learning, to my teachers for helping me learn, and to my wonderful family and friends for their support.—MF

ALPHA BOOKS

Published by the Penguin Group

Penguin Group (USA) Inc., 375 Hudson Street, New York, New York 10014, USA

Penguin Group (Canada), 90 Eglinton Avenue East, Suite 700, Toronto, Ontario M4P 2Y3, Canada (a division of Pearson Penguin Canada Inc.)

Penguin Books Ltd., 80 Strand, London WC2R 0RL, England

Penguin Ireland, 25 St. Stephen's Green, Dublin 2, Ireland (a division of Penguin Books Ltd.)

Penguin Group (Australia), 250 Camberwell Road, Camberwell, Victoria 3124, Australia (a division of Pearson Australia Group Pty. Ltd.)

Penguin Books India Pvt. Ltd., 11 Community Centre, Panchsheel Park, New Delhi—110 017, India

Penguin Group (NZ), 67 Apollo Drive, Rosedale, North Shore, Auckland 1311, New Zealand (a division of Pearson New Zealand Ltd.)

Penguin Books (South Africa) (Pty.) Ltd., 24 Sturdee Avenue, Rosebank, Johannesburg 2196, South Africa

Penguin Books Ltd., Registered Offices: 80 Strand, London WC2R 0RL, England

Copyright © 2010 by Victoria Costello

International Standard Book Number: 978-1-61564-016-4
Library of Congress Catalog Card Number: 2010906821

12   11   10   8   7   6   5   4   3   2   1

Interpretation of the printing code: The rightmost number of the first series of numbers is the year of the book's printing; the rightmost number of the second series of numbers is the number of the book's printing. For example, a printing code of 10-1 shows that the first printing occurred in 2010.

Printed in the United States of America

Note: This publication contains the opinions and ideas of its authors. It is intended to provide helpful and informative material on the subject matter covered. It is sold with the understanding that the authors and publisher are not engaged in rendering professional services in the book. If the reader requires personal assistance or advice, a competent professional should be consulted.

The authors and publisher specifically disclaim any responsibility for any liability, loss, or risk, personal or otherwise, which is incurred as a consequence, directly or indirectly, of the use and application of any of the contents of this book.

Most Alpha books are available at special quantity discounts for bulk purchases for sales promotions, premiums, fund-raising, or educational use. Special books, or book excerpts, can also be created to fit specific needs.

For details, write: Special Markets, Alpha Books, 375 Hudson Street, New York, NY 10014.

Publisher: *Marie Butler-Knight*
Associate Publisher: *Mike Sanders*
Senior Managing Editor: *Billy Fields*
Senior Acquisitions Editor: *Paul Dinas*
Senior Development Editor: *Phil Kitchel*
Senior Production Editor: *Janette Lynn*

Copy Editor: *Jan Zoya*
Cover Designer: *Kurt Owens*
Book Designers: *William Thomas, Rebecca Batchelor*
Indexer: *Johnna VanHoose Dinse*
Layout: *Brian Massey*
Proofreader: *John Etchison, Laura Caddell*

Contents

Introduction

A 20-something man stands in a long line waiting for his bagel and coffee when a young woman enters the coffee shop dressed to the nines. They exchange a smile. He gives her his place in line and strikes up a conversation. Which came first?

- The sight of the sexy woman

- The testosterone rushing through his bloodstream

The answer, of course, is A and B. There's no doubt an average 20-something male has much higher everyday levels of the male sex hormone testosterone than, say, the girl his age, or his 50-something father. Before you finish *The Complete Idiot's Guide to the Chemistry of Love*, you'll also know ...

- What times of day his testosterone level is highest and why.

- How and why her testosterone and estrogen levels fluctuate to shape her response to him.

- Why her brain is planning the wedding; his brain is in lust.

- The chemicals that make him cheat or commit.

- Their changed chemistries if they make it for two years, seven years, and longer.

- Her Mommy brain, his Daddy brain.

- How his and her chemistry change for work, friends, and in-laws.

What makes this new science fun and exciting is the fact that we can now measure, photograph, and understand the chemical interactions that shape every kind of human relationship.

Why do you need to know this stuff? Because biochemistry is the key that turns our love lives into stories of joy or heartbreak. What you don't know puts you at a disadvantage in the game of love. From that first glance, to the familiar gaze of a mature couple, this book will cover the chemistry of love in every stage of life, from the passing to the most enduring. The latest research in sexual desire and arousal is simplified and summarized to help you get a few steps ahead of the chemistry that can make or break your most intimate relationships.

This is the story of who we are at our most basic and most complex, the bonds and fissures of family life, work, and friendship, it's all chemistry, and now, at last, it's all knowable. Prepare to be amazed. Get ready for better sex and more fulfilling love relationships and friendships.

How to Use This Book

This book is divided into four parts:

Part 1, Phases of Love, is your primer on the neuroscience of relationships. In other words, we dig into how love works from the level of cells on up to your brain—the most important sex organ in your body. You'll meet the whole cast of characters: the hormones, neurotransmitters, sense receptors, and essential body systems that can turn a spark of desire into a night (or a lifetime) of love and passion. You'll see how the latest research by sexologists and psychologists is solving some of the mysteries of love that have eluded scientists and poets alike for many thousands of years.

In **Part 2, Sex Is What We Do,** we discuss the differences between male and female love chemistry. We talk about how it begins with the hormonal surges of adolescence. Then we turn to how all that teenage drama sets the patterns for the adult love relationships and same-sex friendships to follow. From our discussion of male and female sex cycles, you'll learn the best and worst days for love, and you'll know why.

Part 3, Enhancers and Detractors, takes on the myths and realities surrounding foods, drinks, animal parts, and lifestyle choices that can either help or hurt a healthy sex life (or, in some cases, do nothing). Apples as an aphrodisiac? You betcha. Stress as a libido killer? Not always. Expect lots of surprises in this part on the folklore and science debunking what's good or bad for sex.

Part 4, Friends, Foes, and Family, is where you find out how and why the same chemistry that keeps love so interesting also shapes who you are at work, in your family, and at play. Ever wonder why two women can be fierce competitors when vying for the same guy, but not if they're fighting over the same job or parking space? Or what makes any two parents fall head over heels for their newborn baby? It's because chemistry is life. After reading this part, you'll dazzle family and friends with the inside story on all of your important relationships.

Extra Features

The Complete Idiot's Guide to the Chemistry of Love also includes the following sidebars.

DEFINITION

Key words and phrases defined. Body systems and brain functions demystified to see how it all works together.

POINTER

Insights from brain and body chemistry to help with your relationships.

TURN-OFF

Warnings about how your body can send mixed messages if you don't understand how your chemistry can help or hurt intimacy and desire.

SEXY FACT

From the enticement used by Napoleon's mistress to new research revealing top turn-ons for co-eds, science is put to good use in these fascinating tidbits.

Acknowledgments

Maryanne Fisher, Ph.D., acknowledges the support of Saint Mary's University and the people who helped make this book happen, including her co-author Victoria. She thanks her friends, sister, and parents, some of whom she visited while working on this book, for their support. She also thanks Tony for his encouragement over the years.

Victoria Costello acknowledges the National Association of Science Writers for its 2009 Science Writers Fellowship, which enabled her to attend its international conference in London and conduct psychological research in England and Ireland.

She also thanks her friends and family, especially Tom, for their support when deadlines have loomed large. For the important things … good food, a willing ear, clean sheets.

Trademarks

All terms mentioned in this book that are known to be or are suspected of being trademarks or service marks have been appropriately capitalized. Alpha Books and Penguin Group (USA) Inc. cannot attest to the accuracy of this information. Use of a term in this book should not be regarded as affecting the validity of any trademark or service mark.

Phases of Love

Where literature has failed to make sense of love, it appears that science is ready to fill in some of the gaps. As hard as it is to imagine a blood or saliva test, even a brain scan, bettering Shakespeare or Shelley at interpreting the human heart, it appears that some of the newest tools and research breakthroughs have given science the edge.

In the first seven chapters, we introduce the complete cast of players and the stage where all the actions and reactions take place in this thing we call love. To capture this remarkable drama, we travel through the human body as you may never have seen it before: from the inner recesses of the brain to the farthest nerve endings of our fingers and toes.

The real stars of the show are the multi-talented chemicals who give us lust and infatuation, love and commitment. There are household names among them: certainly estrogen and testosterone, hormones we've known about since junior-high biology class. But there are less-well-known players to dazzle you, too, the neurochemicals whose effect on every part and process of our bodies shape how we think, feel, and love.

Heart, Head, and ... Glands

In This Chapter

- The instincts behind attractiveness
- How scientists know what they know about love and sex
- Why sex continues after reproduction ceases
- The evolutionary reasons for cheating

He calls every night, and you're crazy about him, but what might change if you sleep together? After a year with her, you thought things were fine, but then she left you for that loser with a big motorcycle; how long will it take to get over her? A couple celebrates their seventh wedding anniversary and both say the marriage is good; so why is he watching online porn while she fantasizes about a guy at the gym?

In this chapter, we begin our search for the biochemical pathways that turn our love lives into tales of happiness or heartbreak. We're going to take on the chemistry of these emotions that have the power to take us so high and so low. But first, we'll see how two other branches of science explain why we love the way we do.

Evolutionary Attractions

The study of human evolution tells us that, as much as people believe they're light-years beyond caveman and cavewoman behavior, three little words are in order: *not so fast*. When it comes to mating, the basic human instinct of *sexual selection* wields far more influence than people realize over their choices and actions. It determines who someone finds beautiful or handsome. And it explains why a man or woman might risk a perfectly good marriage for a tryst.

DEFINITION

Sexual selection was coined by Charles Darwin at the same time he came up with natural selection (survival of the fittest). Humans instinctively strive not just to survive but to breed. And just like other animals, humans compete with other members of their own species to get the best mate.

Men's Drive to Mate

When a young man is glued to a magazine filled with photos of naked women, he's not just being entertained; he's following his basic instinctual drive to play the field. Lust is the impetus, but it's evolution that directs his eye to the female with the shapeliest curves and the biggest breasts. This voluptuous female, his caveman brain tells him, is healthy, so she's likely to be fertile. As an alpha male, he wants his genes, not the other guy's, to live on.

Nonsense, you say—this is not the Stone Age. But in this very core aspect of human behavior, it may as well be. Although, as a species, we've developed other compensating behaviors, that doesn't mean these instinctual drives that have been around for anywhere from 10,000 to 2 million years are gone. They are not.

In one study led by evolutionary psychologist David Buss, researchers questioned over 10,000 people in 37 countries about the qualities they sought in a potential mate. Although both sexes rated honesty and kindness as the two most important qualities in a significant other, the majority of men put a woman's youth and beauty near the top of their lists. Women went in a slightly different, but equally instinctual direction.

Women and Attraction to "The One"

Females in the same international study said they rated a man's wealth and status near the top of their lists when choosing their mate. This was true of women earning a medium or high salary, as well as those who earned less. (Ample finances did not rate high on men's list of qualities sought in a woman.)

No matter how politically incorrect these results may be, numerous studies have yielded the same outcomes. As men value a woman's physical attributes, women place a high priority on a man's resources, or his ability to acquire them.

What does it mean for young lovers on the make today? When a shirtless, well-muscled young man jogs by a young woman at the park, this is why her "lower brain" causes her to focus on his strength and endurance. These are the qualities that are more likely to make him a good "hunter." In the most basic part of her mind, she figures a mate like that will enable her to focus on nursing her young and foraging for eatable plants (granted, at the supermarket), while he brings home the bacon.

Blame It on the Brain

Scientists have identified differences in the structure and neurological pathways of men's and women's brains that support and explain these instinctual preferences. Using today's brain scanners, they've discovered that the male brain devotes more of its basic wiring to visual tasks, the better to evaluate the female body. The female brain has more circuits devoted to memory; this is evolutionarily important so she can remember behaviors that can predict whether a guy will not only generate resources but share them, too.

Here's what it boils down to: even if you don't expect to have children, these instincts that are designed to keep the human species going are still shaping your behavior. Better to understand their impact than try to deny them. There's more on the evolutionary aspects of mating and dating in Chapter 2.

SEXY FACT

Oxytocin, the bonding hormone that helps build love relationships and sustain family ties, exists in all mammals, providing evidence of its ancient and continuing importance to survival and reproduction.

The Psychology of Love

Obviously, our instincts don't tell the whole story of our modern love lives. There is *something* that separates us from the animals, after all. Psychology brings another vitally important perspective to the chemistry of love. It looks at the science of the brain and human behavior, especially our relationships from childhood to adulthood.

When two people find the "one" and decide to get married, their happiness gets hitched to someone else's chemistry *and* to the experiences and expectations that person brings to their relationships. Some psychologists call this a person's "love map," as it consists of all the events, people, and places that have formed a man or woman's basic self-concept and attitudes in matters of the heart. In Chapter 5, we'll take a closer look at how this works in real-life relationships.

Although the vow most often spoken still ends with "for better or worse," realistically speaking, for about half of all couples who tie the knot, the marital bond is no longer "until death do us part." Although the odds are not great for happily ever after, we have some cause for hope. Divorce rates have trended downward over the past two decades, sitting now at 40 percent. That means 4 out of every 10 couples who marry today will divorce. For second marriages, the divorce rate is 60 percent.

And yet people remain optimistic about their second or third chances at love; the re-marriage rate for divorced people is still around 50 percent, where it's been for several decades. Call it the chemistry of hope.

Psychologist Carol Cassell accounts for our ceaseless optimism in matters of the heart as "a loophole in nature's grand design." That is, even when people no longer wish to reproduce, they still desire and can have the chemical rewards of love and companionship.

POINTER

A marriage is not a feeling you fall into. It's a conscious decision two people make to stick it out even after the initial "thrill" is gone—a milestone that occurs in every relationship anywhere from 6 to 18 months into it.

If the original bliss of new romance doesn't remain, a couple may feel as if something has gone terribly wrong. One or both may sadly announce they've "fallen out of love." From there, the next stop is the marriage therapist or divorce lawyer's office.

What's missing in many of these relationships is an understanding of the underlying chemistry of love, and how it shapes and interacts with our psychological selves.

Chemicals in Love

Comparing the chemistry of love at the initial attraction phase of a relationship to what's coursing through your bloodstream five years into a marriage is like comparing day and night. The problem is not that people and relationships change; it's that people fail to recognize these changes as a perfectly natural process that comes with as many rewards as challenges. If couples understand the different stages of love, and the chemistry underlying each stage, they have a much better chance of weathering the changes. Divorce rates might dip even lower!

Similarly, for singles heading back out into the dating scene, knowing how a new romance makes certain hormones spike, exaggerating emotions and overriding rational thought, could help you stay ahead of your own chemistry. And if you are the insecure type in a new courtship, this understanding just might help you avert a dating disaster.

Wait, you may be thinking, I don't remember any of this stuff in my high school chemistry class. Where does it come from? Although the theory of evolution and the field of psychology have been around since the mid-nineteenth century, the study of the chemistry driving human emotions has taken off just in the last 10 to 15 years. That's when researchers got their hands on advanced brain-imaging technology. It's also when geneticists cracked the master code to our DNA, enabling a new understanding of the precise molecular interactions that keep our bodies humming, and loving.

In short order, neuroscientists discovered where specific hormones and neurotransmitters are produced in the brain and where they go once they're stimulated and released. With brain scans and willing test subjects, these researchers set up studies to define which chemical chain reactions dominate in different phases of love and desire.

Their insights have shed light on human behaviors in the pursuit of love. They discovered, for example, that the reward center of a young man's brain lights up when he's shown a photo of his new girlfriend, but not when he looks at the photo of a nonsexual friend. Then they saw how that young man's infatuated brain compares to the brain of someone in a mature love relationship.

Those studying the chemicals and biochemical processes behind the experience of love have come up with new findings to help people love more and better. For example, understanding how libido ignites in men and women (differently!) and what can interfere with the fulfillment of sexual desire for each gender are vital directions for research in the new science that some call sexology.

Other areas of love and intimacy now being explored scientifically include …

The sensory experiences that spark arousal, and the neural chemicals and pathways that transform a body at rest into one ready for passionate lovemaking.

The physiological causes of low desire or libido, which is cited as the most problematic sexual issue for women.

The precise interactions between "head, heart, and glands" that make sexuality soar or stall.

The things we do when we're "falling" in love as opposed to "being" in love.

In short, we are looking into the parts of our human anatomy and behavior that have long mystified scientists, lovers, and poets alike.

Who Studies the Chemistry of Love?

Despite the newness of this technology and the research it has enabled, several thousand such brain scans are now available for comparison and analysis. Experts from a number of related fields have come together to explore the chemistry of love. Here are the primary players:

Anthropologists with a specialty in biological anthropology study patterns of mating, kinship, childrearing, and social relations in different species and cultures over time.

Neuroscientists study the brain, its structure, and chemical pathways and how they affect other organs and human behavior.

Biologists take the micro view, focusing on molecular interactions between the chemicals involved in love and attraction.

Research psychologists design and carry out the laboratory and field studies that prove or disprove the latest behavioral theories of emotions and mating. These often begin as animal studies and then involve large groups of people.

Sexologists specialize in sexuality research and the treatment of people with sexual problems.

Sociologists look at how social patterns affect individual behavior when people date, and then mate.

The chapters that follow will offer findings from the latest studies by each of these categories of experts.

How They Know: Tools and Tests

An obvious question comes up at this point. People are not lab rats. So exactly how do these researchers measure chemical changes and their effects while real men and women fall in and out of love?

Scientists can measure emotions because feelings manifest physically in the body in discernable ways. Just thinking about a new romantic infatuation can cause increased blood flow to your skin and face, which can show up as blushing cheeks. Romantic feelings also cause the release of a neurotransmitter that diminishes your appetite.

Many basic laboratory tools and techniques are put to work to measure these body changes and correlate them with chemical causes. Among the most common are these:

Blood tests measure hormone levels and find traces of proteins linked to particular neurotransmitters.

Muscle sensors in the vagina measure arousal and contraction responses.

The increased blood flow which leads to a man's erection can be measured with an apparatus placed around the penis.

Saliva tests measure testosterone, estrogen, and other hormone levels.

EEG machines measure electric pulses in the brain and nervous system.

MRI scanners chart blood flow in the brain and other parts of the body in response to different stimuli.

The chemistry of love is an exploding, relatively new field of scientific research. Originally pioneered and dominated by Alfred Kinsey and then William Masters and Virginia Johnson from the 1930s onward, today's research and training programs are located in universities around the world. Using cutting-edge tools and discoveries, those who study the science behind human love and sexuality are seeking to solve some of life's oldest mysteries.

In the rest of this book, you'll find some of the most exciting and eye-opening highlights of what they've learned thus far.

The Least You Need to Know

- Men are programmed to seek curvaceous women, while women instinctually look for well-built, resourceful men.
- Ignorance of the pitfalls of the chemistry of lust sinks many modern marriages.
- Using psychological studies involving brain scans and blood tests, many of love's mysteries may yet be solved.

The Evolution of Desire

In This Chapter

- Discover how an individual's selfish drive for sexual pleasure benefits his or her species
- Uncover the scientific evidence of women's infidelity throughout human history
- Find out why sexual pleasure functions as both a selfish and altruistic human instinct

Bonding in pairs is a universal behavior in the animal kingdom. But the length of time the male and female of a particular species stay together differs from one animal species to another. There is the sage grouse, whose "marriage" lasts for minutes. On the opposite extreme is the albatross, a bird whose males and females mate for life and share equally in the parenting of their young.

Evolutionary biologists and psychologists say that men and women have spent much of the last two million years or so living in monogamous couplings, with adultery consistently going on just beyond the eyes and ears of spouses. Cheating, they say, had and perhaps continues to have an important evolutionary purpose. For most (even today), the research shows these adulterous affairs to have been short term. Even in polygamous cultures, only the wealthiest men had a large number of wives.

Within and between long-term monogamous relationships, we display the instinctual human mating behaviors that have evolved over the millennia. This doesn't mean people are only creatures of instinct. Culture, with its social rewards and restraints, and individual experiences also matter. But inherited tendencies permeate everything we do, including how we love and engage with each other sexually. The ways that these ancient instincts show up in our intimate behaviors are sometimes surprising, for example in the universal experience of jealousy in romantic love. In this chapter, we delve into why certain instinctual behaviors have so much staying power.

Why We Have Sex—Then and Now

Before we can understand the subjective experience of why one person is sexually attractive to us and another isn't, we'll step back and explore why men and women want to have sex in the first place. That's too obvious, you say? Actually, it's not. The general assumption is that people today have sex for the same reasons their evolutionary ancestors did million of years ago.

- For pleasure
- To reproduce
- To express emotional closeness
- To relieve tension

However, recent research suggests that modern human sexual motivations may be much more varied. (Of course, the other possibility is that it always was a more complicated question and we just understand more about it now.)

In a study of 1,993 Texas undergraduates called "Why Humans Have Sex," sexologist Cindy M. Meston and evolutionary psychologist David M. Buss distilled 237 distinct reasons given by these young men and women for engaging in sex. The sheer diversity of their responses supported a hypothesis previously put forward by Buss and others that gives both men and women several different sex strategies depending on their immediate circumstances.

Some of these strategies are saved for long-term relationships ("it was expected of me"), while others are employed for short-term pairings

("I wanted to see what it would be like to have sex with a new person"). Still others are reserved for engaging in casual sexual trysts ("I'm addicted to sex").

> **SEXY FACT**
>
> The chemistry of relationships changes with each stage of the emotional connection between two partners, but the chemistry of sex remains largely the same throughout the relationship.

Although the young men and women in the Texas study overlapped in the top 21 of 25 reasons they offered for having sex, the students' motivations included predictable differences breaking along gender lines. Male students more frequently cited a woman's physical appearance as an important reason for their sexual arousal. Men also relied more on availability of a partner in choosing whether to sexually engage. Female students were more frequently sexually aroused by their desire for emotional closeness with a partner, or, as many young ladies put it, "because I loved him."

No one has ever said choosing a partner was simple or predictable. We do know that the sexual choices we make are as much instinctual as they are chemically and culturally modulated.

The Evolutionary Imperative to Cheat

If the evolutionists are right, men's instinctual drive to spread their genes as far as possible into the larger population is an *adaptation* that prompts them to seek sexual variety. In this regard, human men are no different than the males of other species. If he has two children by one woman and then produces two more by another "on the side," a man doubles his progeny and the number of people in future generations who share his preference for sexual variety. Philandering then becomes an adaptive strategy on the part of men.

> **DEFINITION**
>
> An **adaptation** is a trait that evolved through natural selection or sexual selection to promote survival or reproductive success in a particular way.

Men and Polygamy

Because of their biochemistry, men have a higher testosterone-based sex drive than women. This hormonal difference fuels men's desire for sex, which supports their instinct for sexual variety, meaning their "love chemistry" both reflects and contributes to men's preference for a variety of sexual partners.

What About Women?

On first blush, women, like other female animals, gain little by sexual opportunism. Their reproductive ability and success (in terms of spreading their DNA into the wider population) is limited not by the number of men they sleep with but by the nine months required for each pregnancy and the six or more spent nursing a newborn. Women's biochemistry, like men's, both supports and fuels her entrenched sexual instincts; for example, her lower testosterone and estrogen during nonfertile times reduces her interest in sex. And yet women throughout time, even those who describe themselves as "happy" in their marriages, *have been* unfaithful. Why? The evolutionists say it's because women, like men, go where the best genes can be gotten.

For women, the evolutionary incentive to acquire more or better resources to defend herself and her children from hunger, weather, and a host of other enemies made her seek other sexual partners. Apparently, the Darwinians say, this strategy paid off for prehistoric females.

As long as women were secretive about their behavior, by experimenting sexually they garnered more protection, better genes, and more varied DNA for their future biological descendents. However, it has always been extremely important that women behave secretly in this context, given that they are more likely to be the victims of spousal homicide and abuse if an affair is suspected, and the costs of abandonment with children are higher. Men rarely experience the same costs with their philandering.

The Brain as the Seat of Desire

The brain of our species, the Homo sapiens, is larger than that of our human ancestor, the Homo erectus. One reason we needed larger brains, according to some evolutionary biologists, was to psychologically outwit other members of our own species in order to capture the best sexual mates. Those who scored the most sexual encounters had the highest probability of spreading their genes further into the population. Larger brains were then an adaptation of the human species.

Why Size Matters

What does scoring more sex have to do with a man's brain size or intellectual ability? Isn't that the job of that other male organ? Not entirely. The immediate object of complex thinking for prehistoric men may have been to sneak up on and spear a lion. For the same ambitious young man today, it may be to make a killing in the stock market. Either way, say the evolutionists, the deep-seated purpose of any and all male hunting behaviors is sexual conquest—not to obtain the most money or red meat.

Having more descendents with the superior intelligence to outwit, outrun, and outperform his peers puts the entire species on better footing for both survival and reproduction. And these scientists also say the sexual selection instinct belongs to both men and women. It's only because men don't get pregnant and historically haven't been the ones to stay home and take care of the kids that males have had and taken more opportunities to act on what comes to them naturally.

The Secrets Told by DNA

Women, meanwhile, have had their own complicated reasons for sneaking around behind their mates. This pattern, which many evolutionists say continues today for the same instinctual reasons, has been established by modern social science research just as it was reported anecdotally throughout recorded human history and in our oldest literature. Certainly, evolutionists point out, men's dread of being cuckolded must come from somewhere. They say that women, like the females of many other species, have historically shown a pattern of going outside of marriage to be inseminated by a lover's seed.

How do they know this happens? In the case of some bird species, DNA tests in one study showed that one in five of the baby birds sitting in their nests had DNA that does not belong to the "father." According to evolutionary science writer Matt Ridley, in the 1980s, UK zoologists Robin Baker and Mark Bellis found strikingly similar results in an admittedly tiny pool of families living in a block of flats in Liverpool. In previous research done by the same iconoclastic pair of scientists, a survey of 4,000 women in couples included questions intended to explore the women's infidelity and compare the quality of their sexual experience with husbands versus lovers.

One perhaps unsurprising result of this survey showed that women had more orgasms during intercourse with lovers than they did with their husbands. The interesting bio-evolutionary fact of relevance to this outcome is that the pelvic contractions of a woman's orgasm are believed to promote the insemination of a man's sperm into her uterus, thus causing impregnation. Could this be a vestige of the adaptation by early Homo sapiens to ensure that the presumably superior lover's DNA is the one carried forward into the next generation? Evolutionary scientists say *yes.*

Fair or not, the result of such impregnations has traditionally been for the child born of such encounters to be supported by the woman's husband, and accepted as his own. Perhaps the good news is that there have always been men of both kinds available to carry out the necessary work of child siring *and* child raising.

Selfish and Altruistic Instincts

Charles Darwin's great contribution to human thought was the idea that, as a species, we are shaped by our past. From this, all the rest of the theory of evolution flows. Physical characteristics that made life on dry land possible, such as legs and lungs, appeared in the reptiles, birds, and mammals who were our most immediate animal ancestors. Those traits that contributed most to our survival, such as the larger brains that enabled higher intelligence, nimble bodies, and sociability, were refined and passed down to us through the millennia.

At the same time, the human instincts that reflect and enable these adaptations, for example, hunger and sex, are (for us as they were for our human ancestors) largely unconscious drives. Another payoff is this: in addition to fulfilling basic survival needs they each bring us an immediate though passing sensory pleasure.

Sexual selection has made it so humans are simultaneously selfish and altruistic. So in response to the natural world, our bodies and brains are highly attuned to the requirements of sustaining and reproducing our species. The fact that the satisfaction of our sex drive feels "selfish" is just another aspect of the finer workings of this same grand design. What's good for you just happens to be in everyone else's best interests.

Then Why Monogamy?

So given this shared adaptive predilection for sexual variety, albeit for different reasons with different patterns of behavior, why does any man or woman choose monogamy?

In spite of the consistent presence in human history of unfaithfulness by married women, it is less common behavior in women than men, and it's always been so. Apparently, evolution allows women to opt for either or both strategies, monogamy or variety, depending on her particular situation. For a man, sexual variety may simply be more of a basic core need than it is for a woman.

More men stray, all the evidence shows, no matter how satisfied they are at home. However, many men begin to appreciate the charms of monogamy later in life, once their testosterone drops, and the chemistry of long-term relationships begins to pay dividends. Among the positive rewards men and women can anticipate when a marriage settles down for the long haul is a flood of the comfort and calm-inducing hormone known as endorphins, reserved for the latter stages of love. Find out more in Chapters 7 and 18.

The Skinny on Modern Sexual Variety

According to anthropologist Helen Fisher, author of *Anatomy of Love: A Natural History of Mating, Marriage and Why We Stray*, fewer than 5 percent of mammals form rigorously faithful monogamous pairs. Most apes, for example, are polygamous, while some birds, such as the albatross and penguin, mate for life.

Although humans like to consider themselves part of the minority of faithful species, the evidence suggests that living up to those expectations is not always easy. As evolutionary science author Matt Ridley put it in his book *The Red Queen: Sex and the Evolution of Human Nature*, human sexuality is a "system of monogamy plagued by adultery."

Today's Infidelity

Not all of the popular assumptions about who strays and who stays are exactly correct. Yes, study after study from the 1960s to today shows that men, whether heterosexual and homosexual, report that they seek and find more sexual variety than do their female counterparts. Certainly that's the way the standard sexual narrative goes and has gone ever since human beings started telling romantic and often tragic stories about secret love affairs, betrayals, and vengeance for deceptions both past and present.

> **SEXY FACT**
>
> A classic study (Kenrick, 1990, 1993) showed that in spite of men's generally more promiscuous natures, women are significantly choosier about a man's appearance when it comes to one-night stands.

Lest we believe infidelity only applied to our ancestors and to the modern male of the species, Helen Fisher points to the evidence that demonstrates the equal tendency (at least more than generally believed) of women to seek new sex partners outside of a primary relationship. For one thing, she says, pointing to the mathematics of the situation, every time a man "sleeps around" he's copulating with a *woman*, many of whom are already paired with another man. She, like her fellow Darwinians, says the reasons for women's wandering behavior have always tended to be different than men's.

In an MSNBC.com/iVillage "Lust, Love & Loyalty" poll, 22 percent of married men and 15 percent of married women had had at least one extramarital affair.

Other surveys have shown that most instances of cheating happen three to five years into a marriage by either or both spouses, but the reasons differ along gender lines:

- A man feels dissatisfied with the sexual relationship he has with his wife.

- A woman feels deprived in the emotional relationship she has with her husband.

On one point there appears to be consensus: married men cheat more often than married women—and men do it differently than women—more often, and for less time.

Revealing Fantasies

To probe deeper into today's culturally held presumptions of a male's preference for sexual variety and a female's for monogamy, researchers Bruce Ellis and Don Symons gave 307 students on a California college campus a questionnaire. Their approach to the question of preferences was to ascertain the nature and differences between men's and women's sexual fantasies, presuming that what you fantasize about is what you really want.

They found the men had more sexual fantasies than the women and they fantasized about more partners. One in three said they had fantasized about more than 1,000 partners in their lives; only 8 percent of women had wished for that many men. Nearly half of the women said they never switch partners during a sexual fantasy; only 12 percent of men had never switched a partner mid-fantasy. Fortunately, unless you're being surveyed or choose to share them, your sexual fantasies can safely remain private.

How Reproduction Changes Us

Humans feed, shelter, and protect their offspring far longer than other mammal species—twice as long as most chimps and other primates. The belief that parenthood is as much a human drive as reproduction reflects this biological reality. The ways in which pairs of adult men and women change their behaviors toward each other to adapt to the lengthy task of child raising is another legacy of our evolutionary past.

For example, evolutionary scientists believe that the spike in divorces that occurs in the fourth year of marriage is a vestige of the fact that the most labor-intensive nurturing of a child is accomplished by his fourth year of life. At this point, his parents are (theoretically) free to split up with less guilt.

The preference to live in traditional kinship groups is another response to parenthood that comes to us by way of our evolutionary past. By living in close proximity to parents, siblings, aunts, uncles, and grand-parents, Neanderthal parents got critically important help with the demands of raising children.

The First Rules for Sex

In addition to our characteristic habits for mate selection and sex, our evolutionary past has also given us the ground rules for how sexuality fits in with the rest of human society. For example, human beings as a species have always had a physiologically adverse response to sex with their own biological relatives. This is something seen through-out the animal kingdom. Animals and even insects reared together naturally are more sexually attracted to strangers than to their own familiar kin. Higher primates recognize kin and develop an aversion to breeding with close relatives, especially mothers.

Another example of an instinctual rule for sex that reflects a prac-tical biological need is the taboo against post-partum sex. Mothers need time to nurse their young and recover from childbirth. This practice is then reinforced by cultural customs and expectations.

Morality and Conscience

Sexual guilt is nothing new. In fact, for the human species it has traditionally been very purposeful (if not entirely effective) as a means to curb socially unacceptable actions. Over the past century, anthropologists have discovered evidence showing that, 35,000 years ago, hominids had already developed social agreements and prohibitions concerning a vast number of behaviors, many of them sexual. Rules, rituals, and, in some cases, punishments were developed for the following:

- Ages to mark passage from childhood to sexually active adulthood

- Marriage

- Childcare

- Adultery

- Divorce

Morality develops incrementally from childhood to adulthood. Many scientists believe that moral behaviors are instinctual and embedded in our human DNA. As proof, they point to the fact that a newborn lying alone in her crib will cry out when she hears another infant sobbing nearby. Also interestingly, she cries at the sound of another infant's live sounds of distress more readily than she does to a recording of her own cries. Between the ages of one and two, infants learn the concepts of "self" and "other," and they appear to naturally express concern and care for those around them. From eye movements, researchers also know that infants respond to such perceived issues as fairness, bad behavior, and sadness in another person. As they mature, boys and girls pick up cues as to what is moral and amoral by watching their parents and from the culture at large.

In later chapters, we will see how our human biochemistry supports these instinctual drives to cooperate and seek group approval. For example, when a teenage female hears shrieks of delight or receives affectionate strokes from her peers, her dopamine and oxytocin levels spike to reinforce whatever sociable behaviors preceded these rewards. When a teenage boy is recognized for his performance on the ball field, his dopamine, testosterone, and vasopressin levels similarly rise and reinforce his actions.

When morality develops appropriately in a person, he learns to regulate himself from parental and peer influences and ultimately by way of his own highly developed individual conscience. In any culture, conscience is the glue that binds people together. However, it takes chemistry to make that glue.

Sexual Choice and Human Nature

The evolutionary case made in this chapter argues that the goal of most, if not all, of our ancestor's endeavors was not survival but reproduction. Sure, it may have looked as though the objectives throughout human history have been to obtain more money, land, and power. But on an instinctual level, the origins of all these other wants has been the desire to win the DNA race.

The human instinct to spread one's superior genes through smart sexual selection belongs to both sexes. But because men don't get pregnant and historically haven't been the ones to stay home and take care of the kids, males have had and taken more opportunities to act on this bottom-line human instinct.

So it goes, according to science author Matt Ridley. These circumstances have produced the essential nature of the human male, which is "to take opportunities that are granted to him for polygamous mating and to use wealth, power, and violence as a means to sexual ends in competition with other men, though usually not at the expense of sacrificing a secure monogamous relationship."

Women, Ridley points out, because of the same sexual selection instinct, have demonstrated a parallel pattern of going outside of their marriages to be inseminated with a lover's seed. So what is women's evolutionary purpose? Albeit unconscious, their desire, the scientific evidence has shown, is to obtain superior DNA for their offspring, even if the child born of such an encounter is (as they usually are) raised by their (inferior) but more reliable mate.

POINTER

There have been no major genetic changes in the human species since the time when we were hunter-gatherers living in bands in caves and woodland savannah. That means whatever instincts made prehistoric men and women act the way they did—like running off into the bushes for more sexual variety with genetically superior partners—remain our largely unconscious motivations for sex and mating today. So if you want to really know who's steering this ship, get to know your inner caveman/cavewoman.

More Vestiges of the Past

Many aspects of how we go about attracting and choosing a mate are part and parcel of this same evolutionary legacy.

Some examples of evolutionary behaviors with their presumed benefits for human survival and reproduction include …

- The universality of romantic love—to enhance the likelihood of reproduction.

- The strutting, cooing, and seduction rituals of courtship.

- The experience of jealousy in romantic love—to ensure bonding for longer periods of time.

- The higher sex drive of the female during ovulation—to give the sperm a better shot at impregnation.

- The secrecy of a woman's fertile times of the month—to entice the male partner to stick around and protect "his" woman from impregnation by other men.

- The lower fertility of mothers while nursing—to enable her to devote her body and attention to the needs of the newborn, and not impregnate too soon.

- The four- to seven-year average length for marriage—sufficient time to rear a child from infancy.

- The tendency of both sexes to stray—to spread the "best" DNA further into the population.

Exactly how much power our evolutionary past holds over these behaviors and other choices we make in choosing sexual and romantic partners is a matter of debate and continuing research. What's not in question is the idea that the distant past will continue to cast its shadow further than we can see into humanity's future.

The Least You Need to Know

- Evidence for the significant and continuing influence of sexual selection on modern men and women's romantic lives and styles comes from animal and human behavioral studies, as well as DNA testing to determine paternity.
- Behaviors such as romantic jealousy and the "four-year itch" in marriages are direct vestiges of our evolutionary past.
- As a result of evolutionary drives, modern men and women prefer their monogamy with some adultery on the side, although neither is likely conscious of their instinctual motivations for straying.
- In human mating and loving, evolution and biochemistry are two sides of the same coin.

Who's Steering This Ship?

In This Chapter

- How your brain micromanages you in love
- The chemical behind every sensation and mood
- Tracking the chemistry of love through your whole body

We say our hearts are overflowing with joy. Or we bemoan our hearts breaking. But when it comes to love, the brain, not the heart, is the engine that gets romance started. It's also what can grind your next love affair to a halt.

In Chapters 10 and 11, we go much further into how the very real differences between men and women's brains show up in love and sex. In this chapter, our focus is more on the similarities between men and women's brains in relationships.

The Human Brain

You may be wondering if you really need to understand brain science to find a new love interest, or figure out what's going on with your present lover. No, you don't. (People get away with it all the time!) But it's like driving a car without looking under the hood. Sure, you can do it. It's just that as soon as it breaks down, you're going to wish you knew a thing or two about how it operates.

The Brain in Love

In casual speech, we use the terms left brain and right brain as short-hand to accord a gender to each hemisphere of the brain's main processing center, called its cerebral or frontal cortex. The left side of the frontal cortex is associated with the male. It does the rational and analytical tasks. It worries about details, planning, directions, and how something is designed and constructed, whether a city or a computer. In the chemistry of love, the left hemisphere monitors and manages your relationships. It weighs in on important decisions: whether to accept a date, jump into bed, or say "I do."

The right hemisphere of the frontal cortex, associated with all things female, is given over to creativity, feelings, the overview or gestalt of a situation rather than the details, and to awareness of self and others. It processes the emotions of love and prompts you to act on them. Brain science has finally caught up with this common wisdom in at least one respect: particularly in matters of love and sex, male and female brains are *not the same.*

Brain scans done since the 1990s provide photographic evidence of the greater reliance by men and women on opposite brain hemi-spheres, even when doing the same task. Of course, to varying degrees, men and women regularly use both sides of the brain. Renaissance man Leonardo Da Vinci—that multitalented genius who painted the *Mona Lisa* when he wasn't working on his design for a flying machine—had plenty of activity going on in both sides of his brain. The good news is we're all a little like Leonardo, at least in this one respect. Remember that when your next argument convinces you that you and your partner really do come from different planets.

Reptilian Love

As much as we may wish to identify exclusively with our higher "thinking" brains, when it comes to love, and especially sex, the lower or *reptilian brain* calls many of the shots. That's because it con-trols the autonomic nervous system of the body. This is the system that operates largely without conscious thought. That includes the mating instinct, and the biochemical actions and reactions that make mating possible.

DEFINITION

The **reptilian brain** is the oldest part of the brain and keeps the body and species going, directing sleeping, breathing, eating, blood circulation, and mating. And yes, the name comes from its resemblance to the brains of reptiles that preceded mammals and lived some 200 million years ago.

Of the many parts of the lower brain involved in the chemistry of love, four are key for what we cover in this chapter.

The hypothalamus is called the brain's sex and pleasure center because it's the seat or central control station for the body's autonomic nervous system. It regulates hunger, thirst, body temperature, ovulation in females, and libido in both sexes. As such, it is the relay station between the endocrine system (glands, hormones) and the central nervous system (the brain and the spinal cord); thus it's the hypothalamus that's charged with sending out the signal for the sex hormones to get going.

Given the fact that many different drives are regulated by the hypothalamus, it makes sense that you don't want to eat dinner and have sex at the same time. How much can any organ do at once?!

The hypothalamus sends out signals to other organs and body systems in two distinct ways: by sending electrical pulses as neurotransmitters into the CNS, the central nervous system, and by activating the pituitary to release hormones into the bloodstream.

The thalamus is the part of the lower brain that processes sensations received from several sensory organs (sight, taste, hearing, balance) and sends signals on to the frontal cortex.

The pituitary is a gland in the endocrine system situated next to the hypothalamus. It is the body's main hormone factory, including the sex hormones.

The amygdalae are an almond-shaped cell group in the brain. Considered the seat of our emotions, the amygdalae are closely linked by nerve pathways to the areas of the hypothalamus and thalamus that respond to sense perceptions and control the different physical changes activated by romantic attraction and attachment, such as pulse rate and muscle contractions. This ensures that our feelings and physical reactions are closely linked, no matter which occurs first.

Brain Chemistry

Hormones and neurotransmitters go together like a horse and carriage in one important respect: in the chemistry of love, one cannot go very far without the other. Both can be considered "information molecules" in that they carry signals to cells throughout the body.

Hormones, the workhorses of human love and sexuality, are controlled by the hypothalamus and pituitary gland in the lower brain. There are hormones to stimulate and cool sexual desire. Another hormone gives you the urge to cuddle. And two others work by turning an orgasm into an ecstatic experience.

Neurotransmitters are the messengers carrying electrical pulses through a maze of synapses in the brain and through the body's central nervous system. These signals can be either excitatory or inhibiting as neurotransmitters excite or calm the senses. They also put the body on alert. They control the brain's reward center. They signal major organs to get busy or relax.

The Nervous System

The central nervous system is one of two main thoroughfares for the body's messengers and messages. Its neurons or nerve cells communicate with each other by passing along electrical impulses. When they reach a destination, called a receptor site (a muscle, sense organ, or gland), these pulses trigger an action, such as muscle contraction or the release of a hormone into the bloodstream. Each type of neuron performs a different task on a different route of the nervous system.

Sensory neurons carry signals from the internal environment (inside the body) and external environment to the spinal cord and brain, such as "it's hot outside" or "my stomach is full."

Motor neurons carry signals and commands from the brain to the muscles and glands of the body, such as "get up and move those legs."

All Together Now

Now it's time to see how the central nervous system works with the lower brain and the circulatory and respiratory systems to "make love happen" between two people. Watch how outside stimuli, in this case the actions of a lover, creates bodily reactions in three basic steps.

1. Your lover walks in the door and you kiss. Sensory neurons (from the sense organs, e.g., eyes, skin) travel to the thalamus where sensations are processed. From there, neurotransmitters signaling arousal and pleasure travel to the amygdalae, hypothalamus, and pituitary, causing them to release their hormones.

2. You are happy to see your lover. Emotional signals go from the amygdalae to the frontal cortex where feelings manifest in your conscious awareness. Other signals from the hypothalamus activate the brain's reward system, indicating a source of pleasure has arrived. Motor neurons leave the brain to activate the muscles of the heart and lungs. Your heart starts to pound. Breathing intensifies.

3. You engage in foreplay on the sofa. The heart pumps more blood to the sense organs in order to further increase sensations of arousal, attention, and excitement.

These are the systems and organs where the chemistry of love begins. Now let's see *how* each chemical operating within these systems affects you.

Hormones Made Me Think It

Hormones have an enormous influence over your thoughts and emotions, especially in matters of love and sex. Thoughts and feelings are expressed through changes in your physical body. Once these powerful substances get into your bloodstream, they tend to get their way. Hormones can be the source of attraction or conflict between two people. They can create an instant sense of sexual or sensual pleasure. They're the reason why a cuddly puppy can make your day. They increase or decrease sexual desire.

There are two common misconceptions about how the sex hormones operate in our bodies. First, we think they are manufactured only in endocrine glands, such as the pituitary, ovaries, and testes. Not true. The brain also produces hormones that travel via neurotransmitters in the nervous system. There are receptor sites in the brain for specific hormones, such as endorphins. This means that hormones can act on the parts of our brains that control executive, decision-making functions.

The second misconception about hormones is that their reach is limited to the sex organs. Not true. Hormones produced in the glands enter the bloodstream directly and travel to the sex organs *and* to every other system in the body. When our hormones talk, we listen.

Oxytocin

Oxytocin has been called "hormonal superglue," and the "chemical of commitment." Secreted by the pituitary gland, oxytocin is the essential ingredient of maternal bonding behavior. It's also what bonds two lovers from the first time they lock eyes and graze hands.

Oxytocin (and vasopressin) are peptide hormones in that they are made of small proteins. Oxytocin travels in two ways: in the bloodstream and as electric pulses moving through the nervous system. In the nervous system, oxytocin functions by activating specific oxytocin receptors on other cells. Because it has two pathways through which it can travel, this allows for large-scale coordination by the receptor cells in the brain and elsewhere in the body, a dynamic that accounts for oxytocin's sizeable effects in the chemistry of love.

Its impact on us is mostly positive. Fueled by touch and other forms of connection, oxytocin reduces stress and anxiety and aids relaxation and healing. At high levels, it also makes someone forgetful, and diminishes reason.

If you and your sweetheart hold hands, your oxytocin levels rise. If you're in the process of falling in love, just thinking about him will raise your oxytocin level.

Women have more oxytocin in their bodies than men. But after a man is hooked, usually during the "falling in love" stage of a new relationship, his level of oxytocin goes up and his testosterone decreases. This enables his softer side to emerge and aid emotional bonding. Its role in fostering a bond between two people prompts some to call oxytocin the "chemical of commitment."

Testosterone

Testosterone is made by the testes in men and by the adrenal glands in both women and men. Like estrogen, testosterone is a steroid hormone composed of fats related to cholesterol. Steroid hormones are regulated by concerted work between the hypothalamus and the pituitary gland, and released by the pituitary into the bloodstream.

Testosterone's role in turning a male baby into a man starts in the womb. It cues a male fetus to develop a body and brain more like Dad's, and less like his sister's. Testosterone is present in men's and women's bodies; there's just 20 times more of it in an adult male (up to around age 50) compared to an average female. Men produce testosterone primarily in the testes. Women make it in the adrenal gland and in the ovaries. Men and women tend to use testosterone differently.

Testosterone is all about aggression, assertiveness, and competitiveness. It's the aggressive agent in sex, sport, conversation, road rage, and war. In *The Female Brain*, neuro-psychiatrist Louann Brizendine called testosterone "an unfeeling, focused, and forceful seducer with no time for cuddling."

Testosterone, like its female twin, estrogen, impacts the brain by binding to receptors in nerve cells, which enables it to bring messages to the brain's attention—messages like "sex now!" In the chemistry of love, testosterone is another word for lust. It fuels desire in men and women. It's what makes a man walk up to an attractive woman he's never seen before at a party and say, "You look familiar—have we met?" And it's what makes her think, "Gee, maybe," and pursue him right back.

Some neuroscientists believe that testosterone in women is not as volatile or as susceptible to environmental triggers (like a competitor) as it is in men's bodies. Researchers at the University of Chicago and Northwestern conducted a study of 500 graduate business students. Results reported in 2009 showed that women with higher testosterone levels take more risks and are more likely to choose a finance career than women with low testosterone levels. But testosterone levels made no difference in men's career choices in the study.

Such a study does not establish cause and effect—does working at a demanding and competitive job increase a woman's testosterone level, or does a woman with higher testosterone gravitate to such a profession? However, it does make for a fascinating observation.

Estrogen

Estrogen produces a feeling of calm and contentment. It encourages nesting and nurturing behaviors. It also enhances memory. In seeming contradiction to its long-understood positive, calming affects, the word estrogen derives from the Greek word for "frenzy." Go figure.

Estrogen, like testosterone, is found in both men and women, differing only in degree. There are actually three estrogens: estradiol, estrone, and estriol. Men make estradiol only; women make all three estrogens, and each has a different role in the female life cycle.

In its basic body functions, estrogen keeps several of the body's systems running well, from the heart to the immune system. More than 300 receptors for estrogen have been found, including on skin and brain cells. The effects of estrogen on females in dating and mating can vary depending on the woman and her needs. In a sense, estrogen enables a woman to keep all her options open. Sometimes its impact is described as sexually receptive.

Estrogen is a versatile hormone that "knows" the full range of a woman's needs. When she is in the mood to cuddle, estrogen increases the bonding effects of oxytocin, the touchy-feely hormone associated with touch. As a rule, this makes women very happy.

Vasopressin

In its peptide chemical composition, this hormone is very close to oxytocin. But the effects of vasopressin are quite different. Vasopressin increases your ability to think clearly. It does this by increasing attention, enhancing memory, and enhancing your ability to regulate emotions.

Associated with male bonding (with other men), vasopressin brings out a man's desire to protect and defend those he loves. In men and women, it makes someone want to act aggressively in order to connect with someone. Sometimes called the "monogamy molecule" vasopressin modulates the impact of testosterone on a male's sexual behavior, keeping him from indulging in extreme behaviors such as indiscriminate sex with multiple partners.

Endorphins

This hormone increases feelings of well-being and reduces anxiety. It also works to decrease the sensation of pain. Associated with the stages of love after infatuation and romance, the release of endorphins can be triggered by the mere presence of an established lover. As such, it's considered the hormone of companionship and familiarity. Once a relationship is past the initial heady excitement, its calming qualities make it possible for the two of you to eat and sleep in peace again.

DHEA

This still-mysterious chemical is the most abundant hormone in young adult bodies. It is considered the "mother and father of all hormones," in that it produces both testosterone and estrogen. It is omnipresent in youth, peaks in the mid-30s, and then begins to wane in the early 40s.

Due to its immune-boosting effects, DHEA has been used to treat AIDS and other immune deficiencies. DHEA is also thought to increase a woman's sex drive. It may also be the precursor of pheromones, the substance believed to influence sexual attraction by way of smell.

Prolactin

This hormone stimulates nurturing behavior, especially in nursing mothers. In the chemistry of love it also has a unique role: in both men and women it produces the feeling of sexual satisfaction, as in "enough is enough."

Neurotransmitters Made Me Do It

These brain chemicals help to transmit electrical pulses across the infinitesimal spaces between nerve endings. They can be either excitatory or inhibitory. Both varieties play key roles in the chemistry of love.

Dopamine

Associated with pleasure of all kinds, this neurotransmitter has been called "desire personified." Not only does dopamine bring instant pleasure, it also simultaneously promotes the anticipation of more pleasures yet to come, encouraging addiction when a person is vulnerable. This is what gives it its central role in the brain's "reward system" explained in Chapter 4 on lust and short-term attraction.

SEXY FACT

Dopamine, the pleasure king, triggers the release of the hormone oxytocin. In this way it ties the experiences of holding hands, caressing, kissing, and, ultimately, intercourse and orgasm to "the one" you've chosen as a partner.

Dopamine delivers the experiences we often describe with words like delight, bliss, ecstasy, or pure joy. Whether healthy or addictive in nature, the source of pleasure that brings a dopamine rush is often short-lived. (The brain has other chemicals, principally oxytocin, for slower, longer-term happiness.)

In the experience of lust, dopamine jump-starts the release of testosterone. In this way it fuels sexual desire. Dopamine is released again at orgasm when it has the effect of once again reinforcing your current lover as "the one."

Serotonin

Serotonin is a natural antidepressant and mood elevator. It has been called the "soft voice of reason" in the brain. Serotonin levels rise when someone falls in love and fall when the person becomes depressed. Higher levels of serotonin can decrease sex drive and lessen obsession.

Serotonin is considered a moderating influence because of its dampening effect on the so-called fight-or-flight neurotransmitter, norepinepherine. Women in general have 30 percent more serotonin in their systems than men. Women also have many more serotonin receptor sites, and less of the protein that transports serotonin. This may be one reason why women suffer from depression more frequently than men.

Phenylethylamine (PEA)

PEA is like a natural form of amphetamine that fluctuates according to a person's thoughts, feelings, and experiences. Called the "molecule of attraction," PEA causes giddiness and excitement during the initial "falling" stage of romantic love. Because this neurotransmitter floods the brain when an initial attraction occurs, it may be responsible for the sensory experience of "love at first sight."

SEXY FACT

The stimulant PEA occurs naturally in the bloodstream of lovers, and also in chocolate. Since ancient times, chocolate has been considered a gentle aphrodisiac, explaining its continuing popularity as a Valentine's Day gift for lovers and hopeful suitors.

PEA naturally lowers appetite, explaining why romantically enthralled lovers suddenly lose their appetites. A synthetic version of PEA is used in diet soft drinks.

PEA works as an antidepressant in both sexes. At low levels, especially after the sudden ending of a romance, it can cause depression. At high levels it has been associated with psychosis. PEA is another neurochemical, like dopamine, that spikes during orgasm.

Norepinephrine

As a natural stimulant, norepinephrine revs up all five senses during the initial stages of attraction. In this way, it helps you court and hook the person you've chosen as "the one."

Its effect has been described as akin to blowing spark into a fire, all action and reaction. Central to the body's fight-or-flight response to perceived danger, norepinephrine, also called noradrenaline, puts the body on alert in exciting or interesting situations. One such novel situation is the presence of a new candidate for romance.

Only by acting together can hormones and neurotransmitters make their magic. Without this complete cast of characters, falling in love would be a much calmer—and, alas, duller—experience.

The Least You Need to Know

- At every stage of love, waves of hormones and neurotransmitters influence your every thought, feeling, and action.
- The lower, instinctual brain acts as the relay station for the chemistry of love by receiving signals from the sense organs and sending out the neurochemicals that transform your body sensations into feelings.
- The same hormones and neurotransmitters that create peak experiences of joy and physical pleasure can, in different amounts and combinations, produce other experiences.

How We're Hooked— Five Senses

In This Chapter

- The visual cues of attraction
- Separating fact from fiction on pheromones
- Which matters more in a woman's figure: proportions or weight
- How you develop a unique "smell print"
- The chemical explosion from your first kiss

Everything in this chapter can and should be tried at home. For starters, surprise your sweetheart. Surprises, like danger and new places, get your neurochemicals pumping and primed for romance. So invite your lover over, but don't say what you have in mind. Remember the number one rule of love: keep the mystery alive.

The human body is a pleasure machine. As you prepare, make sure there's something to please each of your five senses. Include touch, smell, taste, sound, and sight. Each provides a unique entry point through which you can imprint yourself in your lover's mind.

If the brain is the engine of love, the senses are where the rubber hits the road. The more you know about *how* your skin, eyes, nose, ears, lips, and mouth read the signs, the more fun your ride will be. In this journey, your destination is never the point. How you feel as you go along is what matters the most. Savor the way!

Is It Really Skin Deep?

What is beauty? Today's slender models would not have been sought after in the sixteenth or seventeenth century when rounder figures were coveted. However, according to one recent study, only 10 percent of those features considered beautiful differ from one culture to the next. Ninety percent are viewed as signs of beauty around the world.

The value put on physical beauty has strong biological roots. Your "beauty signals" are noticed by *everyone* you encounter, especially potential mates. But not all beauty signals are visual; some are invisible. But let's start with the ones staring right at you.

Visual Clues

Research shows that symmetrical facial features (meaning one side matches the other) are keenest in making someone fit the label of beautiful. According to German researchers, the appearance of the skin also plays a part. They've been using digital image analysis to record responses of men when viewing the faces of 170 girls and women ages 11 to 76 projected on a screen. The males were interviewed and their eyelid movements were tracked as they looked at the different faces and complexions. It was not so much youth versus age that drew a positive response to a particular face. Blotchy skin, or a face with uneven pigmentation, was considered less attractive than smoother skin at any age.

Research by Maryanne Fisher, author of this book, and Anthony Cox suggests that women more readily consider men who have attractive faces for one-night stands, dating, and long-term relationships. They asked 94 college women to rate the attractiveness of men's faces, and then later asked them to rate how much they would consider that man for sex, a date, or a long-term relationship. Women were most lenient when it came to dating, in that they considered the widest variety of men for this type of relationship.

Fair or not, study after study establishes that beautiful people catch more than their fair share of the breaks. This is true on the job, in courtrooms, and in the game of love. It appears that men, because their brains are wired with so much of their gray matter devoted to sight, care the most about visual cues.

Body shape also really matters. The body shape women most desire in men is the inverted 'V' swimmer's build, with broader shoulders and a narrow waist. However, what men find most attractive in women's body shape is hotly contested. Maryanne Fisher and Martin Voracek reviewed the scientific evidence and there seem to be three components: a woman's waist-to-hip ratio, her body mass index, and her curvaceousness (the relative size of her bust, waist, hips, and buttocks). Researchers are still trying to decide how much each of these three parts matters in relationship to the other two.

POINTER

A woman's figure is incredibly important to a mating male, possibly more than her weight. Men are instinctively attracted to women whose figures come closest to a .7 waist-to-hips ratio.

Clear skin and curves on a woman are signs of good health, and thus attractive to the evolutionary man looking for his reproductive mate. And for the evolutionary woman, health translates into a big, beefy body on the man of her dreams.

Here are some other well-established (visual) beauty signals that operate as universal turn-ons in dating and mating, most deemed evolutionary in their origins:

- Large, muscled shoulders and narrower hips on a man
- Man taller than the woman, for both sexes
- Women with long hair, blondes
- Less hairy men—that is, if you're a woman from the United States, New Zealand, or China. British and Sri Lankan women, at least in one reputable study, preferred a moderate amount of hair on their men.
- Women without body hair
- Large eyes, not set far apart on both sexes
- Breasts not too large or too small

With ancient roots in our psyches, the impact of these visual cues is just as real today. If someone is in a dating or mating frame of mind—or even if she's not—and a member of the opposite sex with enough of these "right" features walks by, the modern brain produces just enough PEA and dopamine to get that special someone's attention. This is not to say personality won't factor in the equation very soon. But for that first moment when two sets of eyes meet across a room, the connection is mostly visual and primal.

Body Language

Nonverbal communication includes eye contact, posture, gestures, your position relative to the other person, and even your attire. Some experts say that as much as 60 percent of communication is achieved through body language. Suffice to say, what your body says is at least as important as the words that come out of your mouth. If the two match well, meaning your words and body language are congruent, a listener is far more likely to believe your message.

A genuine smile works better than a frown or a forced smile. Obvious, you say, but there is also a good evolutionary reason for this. A relaxed smile produces greater symmetry in a face. The combination of a smile and facial symmetry communicates good health, thus attractiveness.

Here are some less obvious examples of body language that signal positive interest between two people:

- Frequency of eye contact

- Length of gaze

- When eye contact is broken, you look down, not sideways (in women)

- Body angled toward you

- Erect, good posture, head straight up

- Open, relaxed hands

- Light touches (for most people, but not all)

Here are some signs of disinterest:

- Blank stare
- Drooped eyelids
- Head in hands
- Tilt of head
- Swinging legs
- Drumming finger, tapping foot
- Clenched hands

Once again, there are gender differences. Research has shown that women are more adept at interpreting faces. The implication is that facial expressions have a greater impact on females than on males.

Smell Me, Smell You

The nose knows who turns you on, and who doesn't. It's almost that simple. The science of smell tells us that human body odor is a very important factor in our selection of a lover; some believe it's the most important factor. Smell is also among the oldest, most primitive senses.

The brain processes odors quickly, using fewer neural pathways compared to other more complex senses such as sight. The nose is only one synapse away from the amygdalae, the seat of our emotions, which then routes sensory information directly to the frontal cortex. Among the tantalizing theories currently being studied concerning the sense of smell:

- Your sexual orientation may influence your preference for and production of a particular body odor.

- Your preference for a particular mate may be greater because his genetic code is somewhat close (but not too close) to your own. In double-blind "smell tests," both women and men report a strong preference for the armpit secretions of strangers over those of family members. This seems to reflect an evolutionary instinct to avoid unhealthy inbreeding.

- Oral contraceptives appear to block a woman's natural odor-based preferences.

SEXY FACT

Not everyone prefers a squeaky-clean lover. Reportedly, Napoleon asked his partner Josephine not to shower for two weeks before his return home. The reason? He preferred her natural scent.

So we know that smell is important to love and attraction. It's also clear that human beings have no control over which smells we like, and which turn us off.

The Truth About Pheromones

Pheromones are airborne chemicals and scents known to influence sexual behavior, mark territory, and encourage reproduction throughout the animal kingdom. But whether humans send and receive these sexually suggestive scents is still a matter of hot debate.

Some recent studies lend support to the view that substances emitted through our pores can affect the behavior and biochemistry of others. In brain-imaging experiments, exposure to estrogen-based synthetic pheromones activated the hypothalamus (the seat of involuntary functions including sex) in heterosexual men. Exposure to the male sweat chemical produced the same effect in women.

At least one study conducted by researchers at San Francisco State University concluded that women who wore a perfume laced with synthetic pheromone reported "a significant increase in socio-sexual behavior," including being approached by men. Other researchers questioned the methodology of this study.

TURN-OFF

Buyer beware: Many perfume and cosmetic products now advertised on the Internet and elsewhere as "pheromone-based" are largely synthetic creations with no proven aphrodisiac effect. There is also no way to know whether a particular scent will be attractive to every member of the opposite sex. Clearly, these are early days in human pheromone research.

Many scientists believe that human pheromones exist, but they disagree about the all-important details: their chemical composition, where they're secreted, and how they're detected in the recipient's olfactory system.

In the animal kingdom, pheromones are said to cause an instinctual, almost automatic sexual response called a "releaser" effect. For example, a male pig secretes a particular pheromone in his saliva. When the female smells it, she goes into a mating stance. Although this effect is well studied in animals, it has never been definitively observed in humans. One can only imagine the excitement that would greet any verifiable discovery and bottling of the human equivalent of this animal courting ritual.

The Science Behind Mating and Smell

If humans do produce pheromones, the underarm is where they most likely originate. The sebaceous glands in the armpit secrete a clear, odorless liquid. Armpits only smell because this and other hormonal secretions are immediately set upon by hordes of bacteria. Bacteria on the skin break down the compounds of these secretions into volatile molecules. These scents produce an "odor print" as unique to an individual as his fingerprints.

Any human pheromones (if they were emitted from an armpit) would drift into a companion's nasal passage and stimulate receptors. Finding the exact receptors in the nose that receive and transmit pheromones will ultimately settle the dispute about whether humans have an organ devoted to sensing pheromones, as many other animals do. It would then also become clear whether pheromone receptors are interspersed with olfactory receptors in the nasal passage.

In the meantime, never underestimate the effects of pleasing or not-so-pleasing smells when dating and mating. When you find a scent that makes your partner perk up and get in the mood for love, you've made the only discovery that really matters.

Tasty Love

One best-selling husband and wife team of dating coaches took a survey of men and women and reported that sensuous lips are among the top five most important factors used by both sexes when judging attractiveness.

Kissing, with mouth-to-mouth contact, is universal. Cross-culturally, tongue kissing is the most popular form of foreplay for couples, followed by fondling and oral stimulation of the woman's breasts. Other species do it, too. Birds peck their beaks together, dogs and cats lick each other all over.

For us humans, little matters more on a first, second, or third date than that first kiss—when it might happen and how it will feel.

Sealed with a Kiss

Millions of nerve endings in your brain are dedicated to the sensations of your lips. Add to that: the surface of your tongue is covered with 10,000 hypersensitive taste buds. Is it any wonder new love is sealed with a kiss? But as you know, not all kisses are alike; we're talking about a long, wet kiss, not a chaste little peck.

With the help of PEA putting your brain on high alert, your first mouth-to-mouth contact with a new lover triggers a cascade of other chemicals, causing intense sensations and the emotions that go with them.

- Norepinephrine imprints the image, scent, sound, and feel of your sweetheart into your short-term memory.

- Testosterone steps up to increase your sexual desire.

- Dopamine and oxytocin produce feelings of contentment and pleasure, respectively.

And all this from one kiss.

SEXY FACT

One recent study reported that 10 seconds is the ideal length of time for a kiss. That's how long it takes to get the chemicals of love pumping into your system. So don't waste the opportunity to get your daily dose. Kiss, don't peck.

The Science of Tasting Sexy

Each of your 10,000 taste buds contains 50 to 100 specialized receptor cells. Sticking out of every one of these receptor cells is a tiny taste hair that checks out the food chemicals in your saliva. When these taste hairs are stimulated, they send nerve impulses to your brain.

Each taste hair responds best to one of the basic tastes. Four basic tastes—bitter, sweet, salty, and sour—were identified 2,400 years ago by the Greek philosopher Democritus, and ever since these four have been central to what we consider good taste(s).

Flavor and taste seem like the same thing, but hold your nose when you're eating and you'll quickly know the difference. The distinctive flavor of most foods and drinks comes more from smell than it does from taste. Sugar has a sweet taste, but strawberry is a flavor. Coffee may taste bitter, but its flavor is also all about aroma. An airway between the nose and mouth lets people combine aroma with the four basic tastes to enjoy thousands of flavors.

How does this science play into the chemistry of love? For one thing, you are what you eat or otherwise imbibe. There are the foods that affect your breath, everything from red meat to asparagus to garlic. Then there's smoking; more often than not, smokers smell and taste bad to a nonsmoker.

Eating a healthy diet complete with lots of fruits and veggies is good for the whole body, including the skin, thus affecting how you "taste" to a lover.

Intimacy and Vocal Tone

Universally, when a mother talks to her baby, she uses a higher-pitched tone. With this special sound there's lots of cooing and stroking. Fathers, too, raise their tone of voice with infants and small children.

What's interesting is that it's not unusual to see similar tonal changes and vocalizations when adult lovers talk and interact with each other. You and your partner may do it, too—but why?

Women have more sensitive hearing. They hear high-pitched sounds better than males. Men are more comfortable with sounds twice as loud as women. This is traced to the hairs in the inner ear; in women these hairs vibrate faster. When men fall in love and experience the calming, softening effects of oxytocin in their bloodstreams, they become more nurturing; you could almost say they become a little bit feminized.

Touch Me, Love Me

Touch matters to everyone, just not in the same way. If sight is where it's at for men, touch is everything for a woman. Women have over 10 times the number of touch receptors throughout their bodies compared to men. In a woman's hands, touch receptors are situated closer together than the receptors in a man's hands. From an evolutionary perspective, women's sense of touch evolved to enhance her nurturing of babies, who thrive on stroking and cuddling.

Animal and human experiments with touch have been overwhelmingly conclusive. A University of Wisconsin study of Rhesus macaques, an Asian monkey, showed that when the mothers held their infants near their heart and chest, the level of happiness chemicals in their bloodstreams rose to the point where scientists compared it to a drug-induced high. Studies with premature human infants showed that if stroked, they grow larger and faster than those not stroked.

 TURN-OFF

Women, with their higher oxytocin, are more sensitive to touch and more likely to interpret a stroke on the arm as a gesture of bonding. Men, with their lower oxytocin and higher testosterone, are more likely to view any form of touch as a prelude to sex.

But there is one time when men and women are on the same page regarding the meaning and purpose of touch. During the early stages of romance, a man's oxytocin rises. This coincides with the time when a woman's testosterone shoots up. This intersection of chemical changes doesn't last long, but it accounts for much of what makes falling in love so fantastic. Take the sweet caresses of court-ship and the strong temptation felt by men and women alike to follow their lust as just two examples.

Chemical Responses to Touch

Once a nerve ending of the skin is stimulated, a message goes directly to the thalamus, which acts as a relay station, then to the primary sensory cortex area (parietal lobe). Each area of this strip corresponds to a different location in the body: fingers, genitals, and so on. When a message is received in the primary sensory cortex, another message is promptly relayed back out to the hypothalamus and the pituitary gland, thus triggering the release of oxytocin, the hormone of con-tentment and bonding.

Not all areas of the body are sensitive in a positive way to touch. It shouldn't be surprising that the genitals contain the most nerve endings. But the lips, hands, and feet are not far behind. In fact, fingertips have the highest density, with an estimated 2,500 nerve endings per square centimeter.

Interestingly, the sensory area in the brain that corresponds to the genitals is located right next to the spot reserved for signals from the feet. This could explain why feet and footwear have tradition-ally been symbols of feminine sexuality. And why massaging a lover's foot is often a surefire technique for getting her in the mood for sex.

The Least You Need to Know

- Men are acutely affected by what they see in a woman.
- Women are most attuned to what they hear from a man.
- Both sexes in love are flooded with oxytocin, producing a heightened sense of touch and the desire for contact.
- The scent of a lover has the power to increase a partner's sex hormones and libido.

When Chemistry Meets Psychology

In This Chapter

- How self-knowledge and relationship skills build on the chemistry of attraction
- Which brain differences in men and women set the stage for most communication problems in love relationships
- The common roadblocks to intimacy and strategies for overcoming them

Because it's such a powerful experience, many people mistakenly view falling in love as the one essential requirement for a committed relationship. But if romance were the sole factor determining the duration of a union, most marriages would end in six months.

As previous chapters have shown, much of the power of romance derives from the involuntary actions of our body chemistry, which in turn reflect our basic instinctual drives. Alas, neither chemistry nor instinct alone (or together) is sufficient to make one of the most important choices of your life.

To hang on to the one you love, it's important to take into account the psychology of self and relationships. Most people find out only after several heartbreaks that the psychological work of self-knowledge and the practice of positive relationship skills can make or break the success of your union.

After decades of research, psychologists can now tell us how to make a long-term relationship work. They say romance leads to an active, ongoing communication; a deep knowing of each other's most intimate joys and fears; a robust sexuality; a bedrock of trust; and a set of practical agreements to guide how you'll conduct your lives together. Most important, love must be both a feeling and a decision if it's to be the basis for a working relationship. This chapter gives you an overview of the most important steps in building and maintaining this solid foundation.

Reading Your Love Map

A love map refers to all the characters, places, and events that have taught you what you know about love since you were born. In this grab bag, everything from dear old Dad's crooked smile to the type of cigarettes he smoked in your childhood home could be on your personal love map, working as either a love attractor or repellant. Just as Mom's perfume, or her way of either cuddling or ignoring you as a child, might also come into play.

Underlying these positive and negative associations is the degree and quality of the early emotional attachment you made with your parents—especially Mom. The mother/infant bond is thought to be the most significant relationship anyone will have in terms of its impact on their ability to form a solid love relationship later in life.

Another current psychological theory posits that the unattached choose a potential mate who is most like the parent with whom they have the most unresolved childhood issues. This way, they can work these out as adults.

His Brain, Her Brain in Love

Significant behavioral differences between the sexes are present in virtually every aspect of love relationships. Most of the causes for these differences are traceable to differences between the male and female brain. For starters, women's brains have 30 percent more mass in the connective nerves between the two hemispheres. This one difference in male and female anatomy goes a long way in explaining why women have a greater ability to multi-task, express their thoughts and feelings, and surmise what other people are feeling. It also forms the biochemical basis for many of the communications and intimacy problems in male/female relationships.

A Woman Talks

Research is now proving beyond a shadow of a doubt what you've probably known since you entered adolescence and started paying serious attention to the opposite sex: men and women tend to talk for different reasons, and they process information differently.

Brain scientists say that women's hearing really is more sensitive than men's, except in the lower tonal range. Just think about the running debates that go on between spouses about the preferred volume of a TV or stereo. Then apply this principle to the tone used by a man and a woman in an argument. Which spouse is more likely to be impacted by a raised voice?

Neurologists also say that men see and perceive visual stimuli differently than women do. Generally, men process more visual information and do it faster than women. An exception to this general rule is in reading facial expressions, where women excel over men, probably because emotional interpretations are more germane when reading a face, as compared to, say, a map. The implications of biological and neurological differences between men and women in marriage are manifold. Women are more verbally oriented, while men operate and make decisions based more on what they see. In the realm of couples communication, women are more prone to talk things out, while men typically mull things over alone.

According to noted marriage researcher John Gottman, Ph.D., women bring up difficult topics for discussion with their spouses 80 percent of the time. Gottman, author of *The Seven Principles for Making Marriage Work*, notes that this communication dynamic is true in the "good" as well as "bad" marriages he observed in a controlled laboratory setting.

Women talk as a way of connecting and relieving anxiety. They also prefer to think out loud, without necessarily looking for an immediate solution to a problem. Because women are more inclined to communicate when they're upset, a woman's silence often means more than the same behavior from a man. It may signal her alienation, particularly if previous attempts to be heard and understood by her partner have not been satisfying.

A Man Talks

Men talk in order to exchange information, to solve problems, or, if they're with other men, to engage in friendly verbal competition. When anxious or angry, men will often seek solitude rather than talk, at least as an immediate response. Of course, each person is a unique combination of what we define, both biologically and culturally, as masculine and feminine traits. Your husband may be more of a talker than your girlfriend's more taciturn spouse. And you may be the quieter one in your relationship.

> **POINTER**
>
> When you listen to a partner with empathy, you have compassion for her. You understand her and you don't make judgments about the content of what she says. Because you're not making a judgment, you don't need to agree with what she says. This is a time to make listening your only agenda. You are her friend, not a judge.

We know from other fascinating observations of married couples by John Gottman that a man takes longer to recover from verbal conflict than his wife. That means, in addition to the personality differences that exist between any two people, a husband and wife must also take into account the tendencies of each sex.

A Man Goes to His Cave

Because of the way he operates emotionally, a man needs more time alone to ponder a problem or personal disappointment. This is sometimes referred to as a man needing to go into his cave, to nurse a wound or replenish his emotional reserves. There may not be a cave in your backyard, but you may find your husband spending untold hours working on his car or in the shop. He's found a modern-day cave for his manly retreat.

It's important for a spouse or partner to allow a man time to do this psychic replenishing. However, if it goes on too long (an amount of time that will vary by the person and situation) there's the danger the couple may lose a meaningful emotional connection. This is always a balancing act, and, frankly, women tend to err on the side of too much interference as opposed to giving a man space when he needs to be alone in his cave.

Although not uniformly present, gender differences in communication style and content are common enough to wreak havoc in many marriages. It's important to remember that these differences can make communication in marriage more difficult, but on their own they don't *cause* marital breakdowns. Both men and women alike can learn good communication skills.

Roadblocks to Intimacy

Problems in four major areas have the potential to weaken most marital relationships. Preparing for these potential problems is like retrofitting the infrastructure of a house in earthquake country. Neglect them at your own risk.

- **Self and boundaries:** Maintaining your individual identity as you create an interdependent, not dependent, relationship with your spouse.

- **Money:** Creating a productive financial partnership with your spouse, not using money as an instrument of power but as a foundation for mutual fulfillment.

- **Sex:** Maintaining or restoring a fulfilling, respectful sexual union, not making sex a bargaining chip in a marital power game, but as the basis for an emotional and spiritual connection for your relationship, and a foundation for self-growth.

- **Family:** Building safety, nurturance, and boundaries for your children; living in community with your extended family, friends, and neighbors.

This doesn't mean every couple will experience problems in these areas. But they are the areas to pay attention to if you wish to strengthen your marriage. Every marriage is only as strong as its weakest link, and knowing where the weak links are will strengthen and support your marriage so that when difficulties arise, you have a plan of action.

Falling out of love is often given as the reason when a breakdown occurs within the first five years of a marriage. This is true especially when the couple's original falling *in love* did not include the development of a solid friendship.

If you're at this stage, your chemistry-fueled fight-or-flight impulse is telling you to get out as fast as you can. But if you have a bond of friendship with your spouse and learn why most people take counterproductive actions when stresses occur in intimate relationships, there is hope. You not only stand a fair chance of halting the destruction of your marriage, but you can also take a huge step forward in divorce-proofing it for the long haul.

When Your Needs Differ

Different people have different emotional needs and preferred levels of intimacy in a marital relationship. These needs range from a measure of personal privacy within the relationship to a fairly constant state of emotional and physical connectedness between spouses. This can become a problem if you are married to someone who has very different needs from yours. For example, the person who wants to experience deep connectedness most evenings can become frustrated if her partner wants to be left alone after a tough day at work.

Typically, the woman wants more emotional communication with words, while the man prefers fewer words. The male often prefers to express his feelings in sexual expression, while the female wants verbal interaction and heart connectedness first, and then sexual expression. The issue for couples already married and in a committed relationship is what to do when your emotional needs are different. The first step is to cease blaming the other for his differences, and stop seeing differences between the two of you as evidence of dysfunction. Less verbal communication is not necessarily bad, unhealthy, or wrong; it is merely less verbal communication.

Sex Interrupted

Loving is much bigger than sexuality. Loving does not need sexuality. For most people, sexuality needs love if it is to be fully experienced. At its best, your sexuality is a physical, emotional, and spiritual experience—the complete joining of two into one. At the moment of joining together, sexual loving reaches its pinnacle. But like money, sexuality is often the site of power struggles in marriage. To keep sex from becoming a bargaining chip in your relationship, you need to give it an inviolable place in your lives. And you need to make it a vital topic for ongoing, intimate communication.

If sexual relations diminish or disappear in a marriage, without an understanding and mutual agreement between the spouses, this is a major danger sign for the marriage.

However, sexuality as a dimension of marriage can never be isolated from other aspects of the relationship, especially mutual respect and communication. When problems show up in this area, the solutions must also take in many parts of the relationship. Again, because of its unique power to restore you individually and as a couple, dealing with sexual danger signs must be a high priority.

A Paradox of Love

Here's a puzzle. The things you love most about your partner during the falling-in-love stage of the relationship can in a short time turn into weaknesses in your eyes. The same is true about you from your partner's perspective. Why is this so?

Psychologists say that we first fall in love with what we experience as the strengths in our partner, and then, as we become more committed to the relationship, we react negatively to the shadow side of these same qualities. For example, strong-willed people are first viewed as clear-minded and determined, but as our awareness grows, this is seen as stubbornness and inflexibility. Every coin has two sides. Handling the paradoxes of love is the key to contentment in the relationship.

Proven Strategies

Clinical observation of successful marriages indicates that good relationships have three essential components that qualify them as superior:

- Trust
- Honesty
- Effective communication

To these basics, you can add teamwork, practice, and humor to your marital "must-have list." If most or all of these exist in your marriage, your chances of achieving success as partners are greatly enhanced.

Communicate

The promise of romance is to find blissful union with your beloved. But for spouses to get close to this lovely goal, each needs qualities more closely associated with platonic love, the generous relating seen in close friendships where one friend puts the well-being of the other above his own desire to possess another. It also means telling your partner the whole truth and staying in close communication—just as you would do with your best friend.

Real love becomes more challenging after the first six months of a relationship because at this point you can no longer coast on the initial high of romantic attraction, the period when overlooking flaws is easy. After these thrilling emotions subside, you and your partner must really begin to communicate about some of the harder issues that can arise between you. These must include your most intimate thoughts and feelings. And if your marital partner is your best friend, you can and will want to share all of yourself with him—the good, the bad, and the ugly.

Trust

True love is experienced in a long-term relationship as both love and hate. That's because people are extremely complicated beings, and in marriage a person often projects her internal feelings upon her partner. If a woman is feeling unappreciated in her marriage, she may fantasize about how much better it might be with someone new.

Instead of owning her frustrations and desires, she may then project these feelings onto her husband, and become suspicious that he is going elsewhere for intimate companionship when he's done nothing of the kind. *Projection* is a normal dynamic in close relationships. The goal in marriage is not to eradicate projections but to recognize them for what they are: your feelings put on another. Once you own your feelings as yours, not his, you can sort out what's really going on. And remember, it's natural and necessary to do this sorting out on a regular basis.

DEFINITION

A **projection** is the false imposition of one's own feelings onto a partner. The one projecting then mistakenly believes that his own motivations belong to his partner.

For as long as the two of you remain married, you are each other's lover, principal companion, sounding board, co-parent, and housemate. That's an enormous amount to invest in another human being. This doesn't mean you don't have to maintain a healthy boundary between the two of you. You do, and the ability to do so requires equal parts self-knowledge and active communication between partners. It's also important to understand that you can't satisfy all of your partner's needs.

In fact, it's usually better not to—that is, it's better to be a couple in a wider community of family and friends. Trust in marriage comes from the belief that you are both there to stay and are equally committed to working on any issues that may be hurting the relationship.

How, you may wonder, can anyone possibly gain and hold on to trust for a spouse in such perilous terrain? Commitment is what keeps you in the game, especially when your temporary feelings may say "get out." Mature love doesn't define itself by a temporary emotion. Love is more permanent, and that's why marital love must be a commitment. Without this solid commitment, most marriages will not last one year. Commitment is the essential foundation of marital trust.

Be Honest

Honesty is your ability to tell the truth. Within the context of romantic love, honesty is a deep emotional commitment to examine your feelings and your motives and be totally truthful with yourself and your partner. Honesty is perhaps the most important quality associated with character and integrity. Dishonesty is manipulation, of yourself and others. Many people justify their dishonesty on the grounds that the truth will hurt other people's feelings. Once rationalized, dishonesty is transformed from phoniness into nobility, and the result is a superficial relationship.

Create Intimacy Before Sexuality

Vulnerability is the only path to sexual intimacy. However, for the experience of sexual intimacy to broaden and become the glue for a long-term commitment, both partners must become vulnerable.

The French refer to the sexual climax as *le petit morte*, the little death. They equate orgasm to a heightened spiritual experience that is similar to death. In death, humans surrender their very essence. In sexual behavior, couples surrender their individuality and enter a union of two bodies and two hearts. Not only is sexuality one of the greatest pleasures of human existence and nature's way to reproduce the human species, it can also be one of the most healing aspects of a distressed relationship.

Honest conversation about sexual expression is imperative if you want sex to be a healing element in your relationship. Too many couples are afraid to talk about sex, and the results are assumptions and expectations that, if not discussed, will harm the relationship. It becomes essential that if you are sexual, you must also be able to give voice to your sexual needs, desires, and wishes, and you must listen to your partner in a receptive, loving way.

Chemically Driven Differences

Due to her biochemistry, a woman's sex drive is more variable, meaning changeable and more easily dampened, than a man's. It's also more subjective in that she often must feel strong emotions for a partner in order to become aroused. Other words used to describe women's biochemically shaped emotional behaviors include nuanced and multi-layered. In chapters to come, we will learn much more about these biochemical influences on women's sexuality, especially how they tie to the monthly menstrual cycle and normal patterns of aging.

Psychologically speaking, sex means different things and functions differently for men and women. According to John Gray in *Mars and Venus in the Bedroom: A Guide to Lasting Romance and Passion,* "It is sex that allows a man to feel his need for love, while it is receiving love that helps a woman to feel her hunger for sex."

Sex by Appointment

At first glance, planning ahead and writing down in your date book the date and time for future sexual encounters with your partner might not seem spontaneous or romantic, but it can actually be a sign of a vibrant sex life. By arranging for privacy, perhaps by booking a babysitter and leaving the house or sending the kids to Grandma's, and by choosing to spend your leisure time enjoying each other without pressing obligations or exhaustion, you are honoring the sexual intimacy you value and wish to preserve in your relationship.

At a minimum, every couple should make the effort to spend alone time together solely for the purpose of sensual or sexual intimacy every week. Ideally this is an unbreakable "date" when you can have real privacy, but if this is just not possible, you should make a compromise to do it every other week. Nothing less than this is advisable. With sexuality, as in many other aspects of life, 90 percent of success is simply "showing up." When you both commit to making sexuality a priority, you're making a crucial statement to each other. This simple act opens up the space for trust, both within your sexuality and in the larger relationship.

You can also use your knowledge of the chemistry of love to schedule your loving times together around most receptive times of the month. More on men's and women's sexual cycles in Chapter 12.

The Least You Need to Know

- A knowledge of your psychological self includes your "love map," the sum total of everything you've been taught and everyone you've loved since birth.
- Committed relationships break down because of differences over sex, money, children, and personal boundaries.
- The best strategies to overcome these common differences involve trust, communication, commitment, teamwork, and humor.

Lust: Short-Term Attraction

In This Chapter

- How chemistry makes a new lover irresistible
- The stages of lust
- Which comes first, instinct or emotion?
- How romance can become addiction
- Love at first sight in action

Your eyes meet and wham! Call it lust, desire, or craving: it is the big bang that ignites the chemistry of love. It's what propels you toward sexual connection. Without it there can be no love, marriage, or baby carriage.

Wait, you say—a white picket fence and diapers are the furthest things from my mind when I spot a good-looking guy across the room. That may be so, but according to evolutionary psychologists, the instinct to reproduce still wields a big influence over who you find hot, or not. In nature's plan, it takes two lusty chemicals, dopamine and testosterone, just to free any two people from their instinctual fear of strangers. And then make them forget about their last romantic heartbreaks. Once you're open and aroused, two hard-hitting natural stimulants are released to get you hooked.

This chemical concoction makes a nice girl imagine a tryst with a beefy guy sitting at the other end of the bar. It's what sears the image of her plunging neckline into his mind, making it impossible for the poor boy to think of anything else for the rest of the night.

Without these hormones and neurotransmitters, singles bars and dating websites would be empty, forlorn places. Welcome to the chemistry of lust and attraction.

Love at First Sight

Is there such a thing? It depends on whom you ask. Fortunately for the curious, researchers have asked this question of people around the globe since the 1950s. From such surveys, they know that anywhere from 11 to 30 percent of those interviewed say they've personally fallen in love after exchanging a single glance. The word used most often to describe this experience was "magical."

SEXY FACT

A visual stimulus can be an effective trigger for the release of the neurotransmitter PEA, flooding the brain with a natural stimulant that can heighten the senses and imprint a moment in your memory.

Visual stimuli strong enough to ignite feelings of sexual arousal and attraction for men and women are not the same. A flimsy fabric that accentuates a woman's voluptuous curves is enough to stop many a man in mid-sentence. Watching Rhett Butler grab Scarlett O'Hara by the behind and bend her backward for a long kiss can put a woman under a lustful spell.

The Mating Dance

The chances of a single glance between two people generating a lifelong love may be remote, but the encounter can easily set off enough sparks for other lovely possibilities to occur. Each person may go off to enjoy a private sexual fantasy about the other. Or the initial charge could lead them to take a chance on the real thing.

The Object of Your Desire

If you ask an evolutionary psychologist, this scenario—a brief colorful courtship followed by a jump into the sack—is exactly how the human sex selection system is supposed to work. Like many other species, child-bearing human females are most fertile for only a short period. If a woman is going to reproduce, she can't dither about her choice of a mate—at least not if reproduction is her priority. She has her standards, but she doesn't have any time to waste.

SEXY FACT

Most animals show off to impress potential mates. A penguin preens and a young man sends text messages, but the purpose of these visual displays is the same: to demonstrate one's hotness to the sexy "chick" across the pond (or room).

According to the Neo-Darwinians, the human eye has evolved with a keen ability to spot a good candidate and act quickly on the business of sexual selection. They say a modern man "on the make" is still attracted to the woman whose youthful physical appearance proves she'll be the healthiest carrier of his DNA into the next generation. This woman has shapely curves, big breasts, and symmetrical features. Similarly, they say the modern female has not stopped looking for her alpha male, the best hunter and provider for her and her future children—even if she can support herself just fine without his paycheck.

"Give me a break," you may be thinking. "All I want is a date for Saturday night!"

Which Comes First?

So, you wonder, is it evolution that makes a woman say yes to one man's sexual advance and no to another's? Or is it the chemical release of estrogen in her bloodstream after she inhales traces of testosterone on his breath? Or maybe it's just his laugh, which reminds her of her dad's.

In fact, most scientists believe chemistry, psychology, and evolution are all strongly involved when it comes to why men and women feel a particular sexual attraction. Just as science has ceased drawing lines between nature and nurture, and between the mind and the body, the view gaining widest acceptance in the study of human love and sexuality considers the body and mind as one big feedback loop.

In other words, the chemistry of attraction doesn't happen in a void. These chemicals are secreted in response to environmental and cultural triggers in the context of who you are as a whole person.

Let's take a closer look at how the chemistry of lust gets things going if and when Mr. or Ms. Right comes along.

The Chemical Punch of Attraction

A woman in an elevator smiles at a guy who's exactly her type, and he asks her out for a drink. They sit in a bar for hours, talking, laughing, and staring into each other's eyes. The next day she can't stop thinking about him. He has lots of energy but no appetite. There are butterflies in her stomach whenever the phone rings. And each wants to see the other again as soon as possible—flushed cheeks, sweaty palms, and all.

When former strangers feel this initial spark of attraction and each decides to give it enough oxygen to grow, they are igniting the four most flammable elements in the chemistry of lust.

High Testosterone and Dopamine

Dopamine, created in the brain and the adrenal glands, fuels sexual desire by enhancing the release of testosterone, which travels in the bloodstream. From there it affects different organs, including the genitals, the sweat glands, and all five senses. In the process, it sets off a wide range of emotions.

Testosterone increases aggressive behavior and pushes a man or woman to go relentlessly after the one who arouses their romantic interest. Nothing starts without testosterone and dopamine acting in concert.

SEXY FACT

Men and women who have higher levels of testosterone circulating in their bloodstream are more likely to engage in sexual activity.

High Phenylethylamine and Norepinephrine

After arousal, the neurotransmitters phenylethylamine (PEA) and norepinephrine enter the mix. These chemicals produce focused attention, with a sense of euphoria that can make the romantically entangled pair feel as though they're floating on air and the only two people in the world.

As a natural stimulant, norepinephrine performs its tricks by putting the body on full alert, akin to a fight or flight state. This mindset enables each partner to notice and remember every little thing about the other—his smile, her eyes, his voice—as if their lives depended on it.

Meanwhile PEA causes the giddiness and excitement of this first exaggerated stage of romance. It's what makes you lose your appetite. PEA spikes through the roof during a new romance but it can crash with any sudden endings, leaving you depressed.

The Reward System

Highly involved in the processing of feedback, especially clues about what brings you pleasure, the reward system is what keeps you coming back for more. The reward system involves several parts of the brain, but especially a C-shaped area of gray matter, one in each of the brain's two hemispheres, called the caudate nucleus.

The Feedback Loop of Desire

This reward system in the brain operates in a constant two-way conversation with the body's central nervous system and bloodstream. The messages it receives and sends through the body begin as neurotransmitters. After they're sent out from the brain, these chemicals activate other parts of the body, whether stomach, skin, or genitals. The organs then signal back their desire for more food, touch, or sexual stimulation, and the loop continues.

In the attraction phase of romantic love, the brain's reward system is activated by almost anything about the object of one's lust: his touch, a photo, even a thought about him. The tell-tale signs of the brain's reward system in action include the following:

- Focused attention
- Fierce energy
- *Mania*
- Elation
- Intense motivation for more

Once a pleasurable reward is identified by this part of the brain, it demands more.

DEFINITION

Mania is a distinct period of elevated, expansive, or irritable mood lasting at least one week. It can also be characterized by inflated self-esteem and grandiosity.

Your Brain in Lust

Although earlier MRI scanners took still snapshots of the brain, newer brain-imaging technology has given scientists their first look at the brain as it changes in response to different stimuli. Using these *functional magnetic resonance imaging* (fMRI) scans, researchers have looked at the brains of hundreds of subjects in the early stages of romantic relationships (anywhere from three months to two years), to see what happens to it when under the influence of new love.

DEFINITION

In **functional magnetic resonance imaging** studies, researchers record the brain in "real time" as it responds to different internal and external stimuli. More activity translates into higher levels of blood flowing to a particular area. These variations are measured with different colors: blue for higher activity, and red for lower.

According to anthropologist Helen Fisher, who pioneered the use of fMRI scans to explore the chemistry of love, those study participants who described themselves as being very passionately in love displayed an extremely active reward system in the caudate nucleus. These newly in-love people also had much higher levels of activity in other parts of the brain associated with the reward system, including one known to be a prime producer of dopamine-making cells.

Anticipation Is Its Own Reward

Because of the way it functions in a constant feedback loop, the brain's reward system can make someone focus as much or more on the anticipation of pleasure than on the actual experience of it. Imagine signals coming into the brain from your skin with news of delightful experiences resulting from a lover's touch. Then picture the brain's response as a steady stream of signals going back out to the nerve endings of your fingertips saying, "Great, but don't stop now."

Truly, Madly, Deeply

Remember, with the help of the natural stimulants PEA and norepinephrine, the brain encourages a person in the throes of attraction to pay constant attention to the source of his new pleasure. This cycle of stimulus and response is what can put a lover's kiss in the same category as a drug like cocaine or speed. Both have the potential to bring a stream of rewards, and, if not moderated by the other thinking parts of the brain located in the frontal cortex, both can result in an addiction. It should come as no surprise that this system in the brain is the root of all human obsessions. It's what makes you feel as though you can never get enough of something or someone.

SEXY FACT

After you find a candidate for new love, PEA and the other neurotransmitters direct how you feel as you pursue the attraction.

From a chemical perspective, it doesn't matter whether the object of anticipatory pleasure is a drug or a person. In fact, in fMRI brain scans, the heightened activity in the caudate nucleus of someone experiencing romantic infatuation looks very similar to the scan of someone who is high on cocaine.

Your experience of lust most likely doesn't rise to the level of an addiction. And yet it's interesting to note that all thoughts, feelings, and actions that occur during a new romance, whether you're feeling happy and carefree or neurotically besotted, are motivated and shaped by this same chemistry of lust and attraction. This is true when a pairing involves two single people who are theoretically available for a relationship. It's equally so when a couple knowingly has casual sex with no strings attached. Lust is lust.

Are You Having Fun Yet?

Some people love the rituals of courtship: the flirting, silly messages, flowers, teddy bears, giving and getting compliments, and the whole aura of excitement surrounding their first several dates. Others can't stop worrying about the possibility of rejection long enough to enjoy much or any of a romance. You may know which description fits you best, but you may not know the chemistry behind your strong positive or negative emotions one way or the other.

POINTER

Your attachment style refers to the psychological profile you bring to a new attraction. The four commonly identified attachment styles include: secure and confident, fearful and clingy, dismissive and avoidant, and insecure and avoidant. These styles interact with the chemistry of lust to shape how you feel at the start of a romance.

Through studies pairing psychological interviews and physiological tests, researchers have learned how different attachment styles during the attraction phase of a romantic relationship are mirrored in a person's brain chemistry. Researchers begin these studies with the premise that if someone feels secure and confident about himself and has a positive romantic relationship history, his tolerance for the unknowns involved with attraction is going to be high. In interviews, these men and women say they generally enjoy courtship; when one romance wanes, they move on to another.

In a study done at the University of Pisa in Italy, researchers included participants who fit this description, along with others who reported experiencing high levels of anxiety in any new romance. From interviews with this group, researchers found more anxious individuals often described a lack of nurturing in their childhoods and more heartbreak in past romantic involvements.

The Italian researchers then found two different ways people in this second group tended to act on their stressful feelings in a new courtship. Some craved more and more assurance from the object of their affection—even to the point of driving the person away. Others played it cool. They kept their physical and emotional distance from a new lover by limiting the number of dates and taking more time between dates. Most important, they didn't become emotionally invested until the romance was much further along.

Researchers then compared blood tests of each type of anxious participant (both the clingy and the dismissive) to those from the first, more confident category. A fascinating discovery they made was the brain's apparent ability to distinguish between all three categories of people and respond accordingly. According to their blood tests, those subjects who became stressed and obsessive when they began a new courtship received an extra strong dose of the calming hormone oxytocin.

As you would expect, the subjects who didn't show the extra oxytocin in their systems included the confident men and women who expressed no anxiety about a new romance. More surprising was the finding that this lower oxytocin group also included those who responded to their anxiety by keeping their distance from a new love.

What does it all mean? It seems that the mind (the thinking, "higher" part of the brain) does have some control over matter (the reptilian, "lower" drives) when a person decides it must!

And Then Add Sex

Sex serves a different purpose during the attraction or honeymoon phase than it does in later stages of a relationship. During sexual foreplay (pre-orgasmic sex), nature's most versatile chemical player, oxytocin, acts as a magnet for physical and emotional contact. It sends out the warm, fuzzy feelings that allow testosterone to then enter the picture and persuade two relative strangers to move past their fears and give new lust a chance. It primes a man to respond positively to a woman's light touch on his forearm. And it makes a woman's defenses melt at the scent of his musky cologne or his sweet cajoling voice on the phone.

The chemicals released when two people have intercourse, dopamine, PEA, and oxytocin, reinforce the choice of their lover as "the one." If we were to assign this set of chemicals a purpose during the attraction phase, it would be to give two partners enough time to find out if they're right for each other. In the meantime, sex delivers lots of rewards to keep them coming back until it becomes clear one way or the other.

In the process, sex can produce a powerful bond between two people who hardly know each other in any other way. This explains why something that begins as a simple tryst can quickly turn into a more complicated, even messy affair. Put another way, two casual lovers can find themselves in a showdown between the brain's reward system, which goes for a quick addictive high, and its attachment system, which likes its relationships with fewer fireworks but more longevity and certainty. As we discovered in Chapter 5, this tradeoff between short- and long-term pleasures frequently shows up as one of the differences between men and women in love.

The instant bonding that comes from sex early on in a relationship is in part due to the chemical overlap between the chemical systems of lust and attachment. The key substance these two systems have in common is that old favorite, oxytocin. Whenever this multifaceted hormone appears during a new romance, the effect is to lower defenses and pull two people together.

As anthropologist Helen Fisher put it, "Do not copulate with people you don't want to fall in love with, because you might do just that." And depending on your attitude, oxytocin appears to be the main culprit or matchmaker behind this urge to cozy up and consummate.

Waiting for the Big Bang

Just to keep things deliciously complicated, it's still entirely possible, and by some reports increasingly popular, to hold off for a while (anywhere from three dates to six months) on the ultimate pleasure of sexual intercourse in a budding romance. That is, when a man and a woman feel romance and lust toward one another, but one or both decide to defer the big bang until later.

In fact, some dating coaches say waiting is far preferable to hopping into bed after a date or two. This advice is based on the fact that even before sexual intercourse occurs, an enormous amount of lust-inspired chemical activity is going on inside each of you. From all that kissing, touching, saying sweet nothings, and staring deeply into each other's eyes, you've already got these hormones and neurotransmitters working their magic:

- Testosterone revving up your desire

- Dopamine bringing waves of euphoria and more testosterone

- PEA and norepinephrine making you feel high as a kite and imprinting your lover's face into your memory

- Touchy-feely oxytocin coursing through your veins producing feelings of calm and well-being

The only pieces of the puzzle not yet present in your system are the super-bonding extra blasts of oxytocin and PEA that are saved for orgasm. Of course, how long you wait before having intercourse is an entirely personal decision, but it may be useful to know what these powerful chemicals are doing to and for you behind the scenes.

Running on Empty

You are six months into the relationship and your high-octane ardor for your new sweetheart has started to wane a wee bit. What's happening? Has the chemistry of love gone away? Probably not, but it is changing.

The brain can't maintain the high levels of chemicals necessary to keep the revved-up state of initial attraction going forever. One likely reason is that when cell receptors (such as those receiving dopamine, PEA, and norepinephrine) are continuously flooded, they shrink in size and decrease in number.

The chain reaction we know as lust peters out until the next romance comes along to rev the necessary combination of chemicals back up. Perhaps all those neurochemical receptors will have had the opportunity to regrow as well.

However, if you and your sweetie are still together, the chemistry that fueled the attraction phase of your relationship is being replaced by something different .... Read Chapter 7 to find out more. But what a ride while it lasted!

The Least You Need to Know

- The desire for sex is an instinct like hunger.
- The chemistry of sex is the same no matter what kind of relationship two people have.
- Eventually, anywhere from 6 to 18 months, the chemistry of lust and attraction wanes.
- In an ongoing relationship, the chemistry of lust is replaced by the chemistry of attachment.

The Long-Term Relationship

In This Chapter

- The waning and waxing chemicals of longer love
- The chemical reasons why commitment makes two lovers calmer and more content, but perhaps less passionate
- Why breaking up is so hard to do
- How lovers' brains change over time

Hopefully, you and your partner have made it to these calmer waters and you're enjoying the sweet chemistry of attachment. The chemical profile of longer relationships differs radically from the chemistry of attraction. The two phases may feature many of the same hormones and neurotransmitters, but they show up in different combinations, for very different purposes.

As is true of courtship, there is an evolutionary imperative driving your instinct to settle down with one person, at least for long enough to nurture some offspring. Even without children, there's a universal desire to have the physical and emotional companionship of another. And the chemistry of attachment is nature's way of giving you what you want.

How It Differs from Attraction

If you choose to make a life with that one special person, the chemical reward you see in the rear-view mirror is lust. Not that you won't experience lust again. Surveys say that married people have sex more often and are often more sexually satisfied than singles. But sex and romance are no longer the primary drivers of your relationship. You're thinking beyond Saturday night. You're getting practical.

Another difference: your brain's reward system is not running you or the relationship. Gone are the dramatic emotional and physical swings of new love. In committed love, you move into a less frenetic chemical circuit, a flatter curve. Like attraction chemistry, this one runs in myriad pathways between your brain and body. It's known by different names, including the attachment system, and companionable love.

Chemistry After Lust Cools

The chemical rewards that couples acquire in a committed bond include endorphins, oxytocin, and vasopressin. And the goodies these chemicals bring? Calm, cuddles, and security. Here's what's waning and changing in your chemistry:

- Your levels of the natural antidepressants dopamine and serotonin levels are returning to normal (pre-falling in love).

- Your levels of the natural stimulants PEA and norepinephrine are decreasing, tamping down the euphoria and obsession.

- Less dopamine is triggering lower testosterone in men, producing a slight dip in his sex drive.

- Women's testosterone is lower, producing a drop in her sexual desire.

And here's what's coming on like gangbusters:

- Higher oxytocin

- Higher vasopressin

- Higher endorphins

"OMG!" you say, where's the love? It's in the rush of endorphins that are now flooding into your synapses and bloodstream. Endorphins are chemically very similar to morphine. Need we say more?

Two lovers in an ongoing relationship trigger the release of endorphins in each other. Like PEA, this hormone resides at the nerve endings in the brain, and travels between synapses, pooling in specific areas of the brain to create the peace-loving, anxiety-reducing effect of endorphins. The best news is that your level of endorphins builds up over time in a steady relationship—courtesy of all that good love.

Let's go back to those brain scans. As researchers expected, the brains of men and women in longer-term relationships did not show activated reward systems. But they did show higher activity in two other areas that were not active in newer lovers' brains. Another interesting finding: these areas were not located in the lower, reptilian brain. Does that spell progress? The frontal cortex or "thinking" brain associated with post-lustful loving includes the region where emotions are processed and data is collected about the body's sensory organs, and the region where emotions, working memory, and attention all interact.

Wait, there's more. On top of the calm-inducing endorphins that need only your partner's smiling face to come rushing into your system, the two of you still have lots of oxytocin pumping through your systems from the extra hand-holding and cuddling you do everyday.

Plus, you still enjoy the major chemical benefits that accompany sex. The chemistry of sex doesn't change from the attraction to the attachment phase. If it was good before, it will still be good. Many couples say their sex gets better as emotional intimacy deepens.

The chemistry of sexual arousal and response in each stage of love is covered in detail in Chapter 9. For now, know that you can count on two blasts of pure chemical pleasure with every orgasm—courtesy of oxytocin and dopamine. And that never stops.

Two-Year Syndrome

Goodbye, crazy love. In one large research project, neuroscientists scanned the brains of some 3,000 people to pinpoint the average duration for the first phase of love. They came up with 17 months. Your experience may be shorter or longer, but for most people, the raw physical and emotional intensity that goes with attraction and courtship comes to an end by two years.

Researchers aren't sure why the body's chemistry changes at this point in a relationship. Conventional thinking says that the nerve endings charged with soaking up the chemicals of attraction simply become *habituated*. The result is akin to a drunk becoming habituated to ever-increasing amounts of alcohol. After a while, he has to drink more in order to feel the same high, unless his body gives out or he stops drinking.

DEFINITION

Habituation means that the body becomes accustomed to a particular stimuli and changes the intensity of its reactions after continued exposure. In body chemistry, habituated cells may shrink or disappear if flooded over an extended time period.

Habituation makes evolutionary sense. As human beings we have a limited amount of attention, so if we devote it to things like a buzzing sound, we can't allocate it toward more important new information. It's best to tune out things that are not important and redirect your attention to new stimulation. If the thing you're habituated to happens to be your romantic partner, that's wonderful, as long as you know how to roll with the changes.

Here's a snapshot of some of the changes going on in your body in a long-term relationship, looking at just one chemical in the transition from one phase of love to the next. Serotonin is the neurotransmitter that gives people a general feeling of well-being. At the University of Pisa, an Italian psychiatrist looked at how much serotonin was traveling in the bloodstreams of different categories of subjects. Researchers determined each person's level by measuring the presence of a serotonin transporter protein in each subject's blood platelets.

Men and women in the first group were newly in love. Those in the second group had been diagnosed with obsessive compulsive disorder, or OCD. The choice of this particular illness isn't random; the chemical activity driving both OCD and a lover's infatuation is centered in the brain's caudate nucleus, its reward system.

As expected, the Italian researchers found that people in new romantic relationships had 40 percent less serotonin in their systems compared to a control group. (Low serotonin translates to a tendency to obsess and can lead to depression.) Then also as expected, they found this same low serotonin brain state in those test subjects with OCD.

The surprise came when they retested the first group 12 and 24 months later. Except for those with OCD, all the previously in-love participants' serotonin levels had returned to normal, including those who were still with their original romantic partners, *and* those who were no longer in the earlier relationships.

What does it mean? When the high drama of new romance is traded either for the single life or a more stable version of the same relationship, your brain vividly reflects these behavioral changes. Two people who previously could barely eat or sleep due to the obsessive attention they were paying to their new romance can finally eat and sleep together peacefully. Unless, of course, they get to this point in the relationship and opt out.

TURN-OFF

Because two years is when your love chemistry undergoes a radical change, many psychologists advise waiting at least this long before marrying.

The Urge to Stay or Go

People give many different reasons for ending a relationship. One frequent explanation is "I've fallen out of love with her." From a chemical perspective there is some truth to this statement. For some, the transition from "falling in love" to "being in love" is difficult. They're hooked on the chemical rushes of infatuation. They'd prefer to find someone new and hope this time they can make that blissful state last forever. Without it, they—and the levels of several neuro-chemicals in their brains—quite literally fall far from where they were.

Three to six months into a new relationship (the point when the most intense of these chemical rushes are subsiding) may be exactly the right time to end it. If you've determined this person is definitely not someone you want to spend a longer chunk of your life with, that's the correct thing to do.

But if your desire to quit has more to do with the "thrill being gone," it may be smarter to pause and reconsider your motivations. Your feelings may have more to do with the underlying chemical changes going on in your current relationship. Singles who perennially play the field may be in danger of becoming "infatuation junkies." These men and women covet the highs that only a new love interest can deliver. They seek the "perfect" boyfriend or girlfriend more than a real relationship with another imperfect person.

Only you can figure out whether your relationship with a partner is durable enough to go the distance. But do take chemistry into account when you weigh your thoughts and feelings.

Fights, Make-Ups, and Break-Ups

Without the presence of a lover, there is no chemistry of love. Phone calls and e-mails can help keep it going for a while, but there is a limit. Because of the way the brain's reward system works, you need to see, touch, smell, taste, and hear each other. Your equanimity also depends on your ability to anticipate the next time you'll see each other. Take that away, or remove any hope of her return after a sepa-ration, the chemicals of love stop pumping. Picture Wile E. Coyote going over a cliff; an emotional and physical "crash" is inevitable.

One of the most common reasons that people break up is because their partner is unfaithful. Researchers suggest that there are two primary forms of infidelity, and men and women respond differently to them. Emotional infidelity is where you fall in love but do not necessarily engage in sexual activity. Sexual infidelity is the typical one-night stand, where you engage in sex but there is very little emotional connection. Women are often more upset by emotional infidelity because it suggests that their mate might be investing time, energy, and money in another woman and possibly her children. In contrast, men are usually more upset by sexual infidelity, possibly because the woman could cuckold them by having another man's child and expecting him to raise it.

When it comes to guilt, one might expect that men would feel more guilt over emotional infidelity because this is what is important to women. Instead, Maryanne Fisher, author of this book, and her team found that men feel guilt over sexual infidelity, and women over emotional infidelity. This finding suggests that people have a hard time understanding what might be really important to the other sex.

Chemistry of Fighting

Just as each phase of love has a chemical profile, so do the nasty fights and tasty make-ups that come up in every love relationship. You can think of the cycle of fighting and making up as a miniature version of the two stages of love. When a fight ends one cycle, the act of making up begins another.

Then there's the pure pleasure of making up. The positive chemical rush of getting back together can be as good as or better than the explosive chemistry of your first few dates. Lovers reunited after a quarrel relish "make-up sex" for good reason.

SEXY FACT

The unusually high testosterone in women during the attraction phase of romance usually wanes beginning three to nine months into a relationship. If the couple doesn't know better, he might fear she's lost interest. Seeing things differently after a drop in her testosterone, she might fear he's turned into a sex maniac.

Sometimes it takes two break-ups to end a relationship that's not working. That's because after experiencing the withdrawal brought on by separation, the couple misinterprets the chemically dictated emotional and physical distress they experience. Their pain continues for days, weeks, or months, and instead of understanding their discomfort as a natural process, one that will eventually end, the ex-lovers see it as a signal that parting was a mistake. Their shared misery then becomes misguided validation that they really do belong together. If they get back together without dealing with the real issue that prompted the fights, tensions erupt again. Only this time they are likely to be fiercer because of the pain each of them knows lies ahead if things don't work out.

What can you do to alleviate the pain of breaking up? As counterintuitive as it may seem, the best remedy for the pain of lost love is just to *feel it*. That's right: cry, brood, hit pillows, yell, take a walk alone or with a friend, talk it out, and just allow yourself to feel rotten. Repressing the feelings only makes them fester and get worse.

POINTER

Want to ease the pain of breaking up? Try upping your oxytocin level by increasing other forms of touch. Get a massage. Cuddle with your kitty.

The common wisdom that it takes one month of recovery time for every year spent in a relationship has a valid chemical basis. When you've had the companionship of a partner for years or decades, your levels of oxytocin and endorphins, the hormones of calm and contentment associated with everyday touch and regular sexual contact, reach a set point. Without that partner's presence or a hope of his return, these chemicals begin to subside. After reaching a new low point, they can take longer to build back up to something approaching normal.

Chemistry of Rejection

In brain scans of 15 people recently dumped by their lovers, researchers (again Helen Fisher, with her associates Brown and Aron) found high levels of activity in the areas associated with physical pain, obsessive behavior, and risk-taking. Is it any wonder that people who find the pain of rejection unbearable frequently do "crazy" things? They replay phone messages to hear an old lover's voice. They drive by an ex's house or go to the places they once frequented together. Some are so driven with pain they harass the old lover by stalking them or sending unwanted messages.

More than sadness, these behaviors are expressions of anger and frustration. In the view of anthropologist Helen Fisher, they are evolutionary-based protests over the threat of abandonment. Writing in *Why We Love*, Fisher speculates that our animal and human ancestors developed a panic reaction to separation in order to protect their young offspring. In another twist, she suggests these rage-fueled negative behaviors may also have served to drive the lovers to extricate themselves from dead-end matches. The anger, fury, panic, and even the ability of a spurned lover to hate his beloved can then be understood as adaptations that were once crucial to human survival.

From a chemical perspective, Fisher pins these behaviors on the hyperactive pumping of dopamine and norepinephrine after a break-up. If the desired reward, the return of a lover, is delayed or removed, dopamine-producing neurons go on overdrive. At very high levels, and with help from the overstimulating agent of fight or flight, norepinephrine, feelings of intense anxiety and fear can overwhelm the spurned lover. He then is pushed to act in crazy ways to get back the source of his pleasure.

These reactions, which sometimes result in "crimes of passion," have long been understood by human culture as a special form of temporary insanity. Hopefully, by knowing the powerful chemical reactions that everyone goes through when breaking up with a lover, you can panic less and understand more if and when there's a next time for you.

Keeping It on Track

If you're one of the 10 percent of long-time married couples who pump out as much romantic juice now as you did when you were first dating, you get the best of both worlds. Who are these fortunate people?

If they're truly lucky, they found the perfect partner and they do together what comes to them naturally: in a word, romance. In a 2008 study done by Dr. Arthur Aron at Stony Brook University, fMRI brain scans were done comparing newer couples to married pairs who had been together for 20 years or more. Although most of the latter group exhibited the changed, tamped-down chemistry of attachment, researchers found 1 in 10 of these long-term marrieds who had managed to hold on to the hotter chemistry of attraction.

For most people, keeping passion alive in a long-term relationship takes more than luck. They have to consciously make time for romance and find new ways to rekindle sexual sparks. They must vow not to take each other for granted after years of togetherness.

You Can Revive Your Relationship

If, as we now know, the chemistry of attraction fades for most couples within six to nine months, how are you supposed to maintain a satisfying sex life for the years and decades you hope to spend with your spouse?

Forget about ignoring the problem; it's like a toothache, and un-treated problems only get worse. You also shouldn't expect to find marital happiness by becoming celibate buddies with your spouse, essentially shutting down your sexuality. He's not just your best friend, nor is he your brother; he's your beloved. And unless two parties agree to a cessation of sexual relations for health or another mutually acceptable reason, leaving sensuality or sexuality out of the marriage can leave one partner bitter and the relationship weaker.

Having an affair won't help, either. Diverting your sexual needs to an affair with someone else will undoubtedly produce short-term drama to heat up a marriage, but it's not a long-term solution. An affair, discovered or not, can also aggravate feelings of abandonment or distrust, feelings that may be present already if your sexuality is absent or minimally present.

Finally, simply adding variety or novelty will not rescue a dying sexual relationship. Buying sexy lingerie and sex toys, trying new sexual positions, or even "swinging" with another couple can provide diversion and fleeting relief from the sexual doldrums, but it can also produce more tension between partners, especially if one feels pressured by the other to perform or get with the program.

Any or all of these things can spice up the relationship if the two partners are on the same page and both wish to try something new, but these novel behaviors are no substitute for the one essential step you must take if you wish to bring passion back to your relationship: restoring and deepening the connection between the two of you.

Instead of trying to go back to an earlier stage when the attraction chemistry between you made everything new and exciting, use the chemistry of familiarity to go deeper into your intimacy. By all means, get out some of your old romantic tricks that may have gotten dusty from lack of use. Bring each other flowers, do foot massages, trade compliments. The admonition "use it or lose it" is as true about your intimacy muscles as it is any other part of your body.

Start with You

So you've concluded that your relationship and/or sex life needs a reboot. The way to begin is by thinking of this as a time to rediscover each other, beginning with you. You may have thought you were about to "fix" your relationship, but whoever once said, "Happiness is an inside job," had it exactly right. It's hard to feel sexually attracted to your partner if you aren't feeling physically fit or content in your own body. The issue goes far beyond attractiveness. A poor self-image is the elephant in the room in many dysfunctional relationships.

Too many marriages, and even marriage therapists, regard self-image as off-limits for discussion or confrontation when attempting to deal with dysfunction in a sexual relationship. Whether you're attempting to bring sexuality back with the help of a therapist or you're doing it on your own, the place to start is within yourself. One way to begin the process is to take some steps to gently wake up your senses. Take the time to romance yourself.

Here are some simple exercises that will help:

- **Relax your body:** Sit or lie down on the floor or the bed. Put your attention on every part of your body one by one, commanding each to relax completely. Go from your head to your toes, taking 10 or 15 minutes to release all your tension. Count from 10 to 0, for your forehead, neck, arms, pelvis, and so on, until each is completely relaxed. If you'd prefer to do this exercise in water, find a tub, fill it with steaming hot water, light a candle, and take it from the top.

- **Move:** Take a daily walk, a run up the stairs, or dance to your favorite music.

- **Use positive affirmations:** "I am a beautiful, zesty, sexy woman ...."

- **Rediscover sexual self-pleasuring:** Try a vibrator, get a mirror, and lock the door.

- **"Sensualize" your environment:** Light candles, get a fur rug or a new duvet, hang nudes on the walls, move the stereo into the bedroom.

The point of these activities is to re-open your body and mind to nonsexual sensuality and feelings. Unless you can stop the whirlwind of activity and worry and engage all five of your senses, healthy sexuality, not to mention life itself, will speed right past you while you're not looking.

Rediscovering your self will then extend to your relationship. Your goal is to give each of you the opportunity to get to know the other's body, mind, and heart all over again—as if for the first time. It's one of the challenges of marital familiarity: the feeling that you know everything there is to know about each other. You've heard him tell the same stories a thousand times. You know what he's thinking. There's nothing more to know. But you're undoubtedly wrong!

Proven Strategies to Reawaken Sexuality

One person can do a lot to reawaken herself sensually and sexually, but, ultimately, reviving sexuality in a marriage requires the participation of both partners. If you are the one asking for your partner's involvement in a sexual renewal, be sure to frame your request positively. "I'd like to put more effort into making our sex life better," sounds sweeter and a lot more inviting than, "Our sex is so boring. I can't stand it anymore." Certainly threats and ultimatums are not constructive. Be sure to begin gently; perhaps offer to do something for him, such as give a massage or foot rub.

If your partner responds either tentatively or negatively, try not to overreact. You may have caught her by surprise. She may still feel stuck in the old stalemate. Give her time to process your request. Be positive. Before you interpret your partner's lack of enthusiasm as being a message about you, or your body, consider these questions:

- Is she overtired and stressed out?

- Has she recently experienced a loss?

- Is she just getting over a physical illness?

- Is she worried about a situation at work?

Let her know that your offer stands even if she's not ready to take you up on it just then. Then she can come back to you when she's ready. If she responds enthusiastically, allow things to unfold without pushing or intellectualizing. After enjoying some sensual time together, you may wish to take the opportunity to open up the conversation. If this feels like it would help the two of you open up further to clear the air, then by all means speak about what's been going on between the two of you sexually.

Remember, you're looking to share feelings at this time, not to assign blame or offer a negative prognosis on the past or future of your sexuality. The most important thing you can express to her is your real desire to bring back the sexual passion you used to enjoy in your relationship. And when you talk, keep touching her. It's amazing how much love can be expressed in a simple stroke.

Go slow! Ironically, the best way sex therapists have found to help people rejuvenate sexuality is by advising the couple to *do anything but* have sexual intercourse for some period of time. The idea is to take all pressure off, and keep performance completely off the table.

Sensuality comes before sexuality. Playful touching, kissing, and caressing are what will ideally unfold at this stage. There's also some counter-suggestion going on here; no matter how old people are, they tend to rebel against something they're told to do—or not to do.

So whether you take all the advice or a part of it, your objective is to go slow. Envision what might happen if you were to go back to your very first date, before you ever shared a single passionate kiss. Try to recapture the initial feelings and small steps you took before you both "opted in" to full sexual expression. What did his kisses feel like? What about the first electric spark you exchanged? When and where did it happen?

A long-term relationship is cause for celebration. The benefits long-married couples say they value most are the intimacy and security that time brings to the union. At its best, this longevity translates into companionship with continuing passion serving as the glue holding you together.

The Least You Need to Know

- After two years, your love chemistry is ready to be completely overhauled.
- Be prepared to trade the roller-coaster excitement of lust for the smoother sailing of a dependable love.
- Lust cools, but sex need not become less passionate.
- Sometimes the chemistry of parting is so painful it takes two rounds of breaking up to make a permanent split from a long-time love gone wrong.
- The passion in a long-term relationship inevitably cools, but it can be revived with a process of rediscovery and a conscious effort to deepen intimacy between two partners.

Sex Is What We Do

As boys become young men and girls tiptoe into womanhood, their biochemistry begins a major overhaul, much of it in preparation for love. Over the next five chapters, we look at the major differences created by this changing chemistry as men and women enjoy their sexuality in love relationships from puberty onward.

There's new light shed on the female monthly cycle, and on the little-known male hormonal cycle, which shapes when his sexual desire rises and falls and what he's likely to do about it. There are insights into differences between male and female brain chemistry, and what that means in and out of bed. Armed with this new knowledge, the battle of the sexes just might be headed for a cease-fire.

Growing Up

The teen brain craves drama; a teen's parents, not so much. Along with the teenager's significant body changes come legendary outbursts of defiance and bouts of moodiness. Boys and girls have a shared obsession with the mirror and each other. They see themselves as independent of their parents, even if they can't yet pull it off. Adolescence is a turbulent time offering equal parts joy and sorrow for teens and their parents. It's also the starting place for our love maps and the chemistry that gets it all going.

Little of it, however, is avoidable. The typical adolescent's tantrums and outsized enthusiasms can be thought of as collateral damage in the natural process of growing up. In fact, these challenging emotions and behaviors are the only possible responses to the enormous chemical changes going on inside every teenager's body.

The Challenges of Puberty

For girls starting at age 8, and boys by 10, pre-pubescent brains and bodies begin subtle changes that lead to major transformations in full swing by age 12. Some of these changes are not complete until the age of 25.

The sex hormones testosterone and estrogen are the producers and directors of these blockbuster body and mind shifts. Before puberty, boys and girls have these hormones in basically the same amounts circulating through their bloodstreams. But when testosterone spikes in boys, reaching 20 times as much as in the girls, and the estrogen/progesterone cycle begins in girls, the common denominator between the two sexes is their massive hormonal transformation. And as anyone knows as they look back at those years, nothing will ever be the same—especially not in love.

Adolescence is when we first get to see the amazing power of hormones to alter mind and body. Although a hormone doesn't make you do something, it raises the likelihood that you will under certain circumstances. For example, the blast of testosterone gives a teenage boy an off-the-charts sex drive, which more often leads him no further than fantasies and masturbation. But if a girl's newly awakened libido and her oxytocin-driven desire for touch rise sufficiently to meet his libido, then these two are going to have sex!

It isn't the first time testosterone and estrogen have brought about structural changes in this same boy and girl. While in their mother's womb, every fetus, according to her or his DNA, is exposed to testosterone or estrogen, which creates the blueprint of the male or female brain. However, estrogen is not nearly as important as the absence of testosterone, because girls have the brains that boys would have if the developing male fetus did not produce and get exposed to testosterone. This drenching with hormones causes the prenatal growth of sex-typed receptors on their nerve cells in the brain and on other organs.

During childhood, the structural divergence in boys' and girls' brains shows up in physical, cognitive, and behavioral differences. Girls spend more of their time in bonding activities, and take the lead in learning and language skills. Boys are more active and physical; in play, boys demonstrate perceptual and spatial advantages. Another thing they have in common: boys and girls tend to avoid each other in favor of the company of their own sex. It's the lull before the storm.

Brains, Bodies, and How They Change

With puberty, her brain is programmed so that near age 13, waves of estrogen trigger her breasts to swell and her ovaries to start menstruation. His brain is wired to receive testosterone to order the descent of his testicles and the bulking up of his shoulders, along with a narrowing of his hips. As this new chemistry takes full effect in an adolescent's re-sculpted body, it goes on to alter just about everything else about that teen: behavior, perceptions, emotions, and abilities.

Many signs of puberty are obvious and, of course, appealing. Others are invisible and present challenges. The largest as-yet-unseen change happens in the brain, where millions of neurons and neural extensions are sprouting. The purpose of these new nerve cells is to carry emotional pulses from the amygdalae to the frontal cortex.

The problem with all this transformation is that until age 19 or 20, these nerve cells lack a full coat of myelin, the substance that promotes and stabilizes nerve growth, leaving them thin and immature. That means any strong emotion, especially when any additional stress gets added on, can cause a circuit overload in the teenage brain. This accounts for the impulsive nature of most teens, as well as their tendency to make immature judgments. It also sheds light on an adolescent's emotional volatility and low impulse control.

POINTER

With their newly sprouted nerves not ready to handle outsized emotions, teens have a strong temptation to self-medicate their state of overwhelm with alcohol and illegal drugs. Parents can help their teenagers find other ways to handle the stress of growing up: sports, creative pursuits, time with friends.

For a 15-year-old girl who must take a math final while dealing with the discomforts of PMS, immature nerves may be expressed as tears, failure to study, and a bad grade on the test. For a 16-year-old boy who is fantasizing incessantly about scoring with girls, these same immature neurons might manifest with an attack of shyness the next time he's near a girl.

Boobs and Moods: Girls and Puberty

With girls in the lead by about two years, puberty arrives with a chorus of shrieks, giggles, and slammed doors. The chemical brakes are taken off a girl's hypothalamic/pituitary/ovarian system, which has been held in check since she was a toddler. She begins the transformation into a curvaceous creature with a fascination for boys and a fixation on her own developing sex appeal.

Monthly menstrual cycles are a lifelong challenge for many women. But at the tender age of about 12 (depending on such factors as ethnicity, urban or rural location, present or absent father), when girls' bodies and feelings are still so tentative, the up-and-down mood and energy cycles that accompany periods also begin. It is easy enough for most girls to ride the elevated mood and energy levels of the first week and a half leading to ovulation. With this upswing in estrogen, menstruating girls tend to be emotionally buoyant and intellectually sharper. They're keen to bond emotionally with their girlfriends, and enjoy flirting with boys.

But when they reach the middle of their period and pass ovulation, these young females come up against a sharp drop in estrogen and a rise in progesterone, wreaking havoc with their moods and energy levels. In weeks three and four, many encounter cramps and headaches, along with sudden feelings of irritability and a desire to be left alone. Not surprisingly, this is the peak period in the teen month for fights between girls and their parents.

The Estrogen Rush

Boys' and girls' hormonal flows are regulated by the hypothalamus, which tells the pituitary to open or close the valve for the release of the appropriate sex hormone. But adolescent girls face an extra challenge: the wide hormonal fluctuations they face in the course of every month.

When a girl's estrogen rises, the valve regulating this hormone stays open. This signals the follicles of their ovaries to secrete even more estrogen, in order to promote the growth of an egg and create the conditions necessary for pregnancy to occur. This flush of estrogen fuels those first two high-energy weeks of a menstruating female's month.

If an egg is fertilized, estrogen and progesterone levels stay high. If not, progesterone takes over. Unlike estrogen, progesterone has an inhibitory effect. This means during the second half of the female cycle it slows the blood flowing to the frontal cortex, and lowers both oxygen and glucose consumption. The net effect is a more sluggish brain and all-around lower energy level during the last two weeks of her monthly cycle, with a corresponding drop in libido.

In addition to causing the monthly release of eggs from her ovaries, estrogen and progesterone help a teen girl's body break down proteins and dietary fat, redistributing this fat to other areas. As that happens, her body becomes rounded and her breasts swell. By her mid-teens, the average teenage girl has a new *body composition* ratio of 23 percent lean mass and 25 percent fat.

DEFINITION

In physical fitness, **body composition** is defined as the percentage of fat, muscle, and bone in the body. Usually it's expressed as a ratio of lean mass to fatty mass. Lean mass includes muscle, bone, skin, internal organs, and body water. Fatty mass is mostly composed of body fat as well as internal essential fat surrounding organs.

Chemistry of Cliques and Cattiness

When puberty arrives, teenage girls still want to be with each other, but for different reasons. This is when teen girls form cliques. In these fiercely bonded groups, girls achieve two primary goals:

- They have reliable and loyal peers with whom they can talk about *everything*.

- They help each other attract boys.

There is a chemical underpinning to this behavior. Starting in the teen years, females, more than males, receive the positive effects of higher oxytocin and dopamine from the emotional and physical contact they exchange.

POINTER

Parents beware: when you punish a teen girl by denying her access to her friends, you can expect an emotional crash. That's because girls get an oxytocin and dopamine boost *just from talking with each other*. Is it any wonder they can't live without phoning, texting, and hanging out together constantly?

Even though getting a boy to notice her is one of an adolescent girl's highest priorities, she quickly discovers that it's her girlfriends who share her need and facility for chatting about every little thing. This pattern is one that a majority of women keep for life.

However, not all girls' relationships are positive. As competition begins for finding a suitable boy to date, girls begin to ostracize each other, spread rumors about a rival's sexual history, and verbally insult each other. Unlike boys, the nature of competition among girls often is indirect and nonviolent, as though they want to disguise the fact that they are competing at all. Measuring how girls compete with each other has been problematic for scientists because it is difficult to put a number on a well-worded put down, or on the causes of ostracism or rejection.

When things don't go well for a teenage girl—when a parent grounds her for staying out late, or she has a fight with her boyfriend—there is a bottoming out of dopamine, oxytocin, and serotonin. In these emotionally difficult times, cortisol, the stress hormone, takes over, producing the emotional meltdowns that girls this age are known for.

Still, despite her explosive moods, a 13-year-old girl's emotional maturity and verbal abilities are way ahead of the boys her age.

Boys: "Wow, Girls!"

Beginning in puberty, boys have advantages and challenges of their own. For boys, growth spurts, physical strength, and sexual awareness tend to come sooner and to a greater degree than girls. Boys start to find ways to stand out from the pack and show off for the benefit of girls. They also crave independence and respect from their male peers. Again, many of these behaviors become lifelong patterns for adult men.

The Testosterone Flush

Testosterone in boys builds up their bulk, increasing the capacity of the body to store calcium, phosphorus, and other elements essential to the growth and repair of bones and muscles.

Testosterone rivets boys' thoughts and emotions to the subject of sex. Given the chance, teenage boys will spend hours each day ogling girls' bodies—in person, in print, or onscreen. With a steady stream of the male sex hormone flowing through their brains and bodies, not fluctuating as estrogen does in a girl's monthly cycle, teenage boys are basically horny all the time.

Boys' sexuality differs from girls' from the start. Whereas affection and touching is enough for most girls at this age, the teen boy's skyrocketing testosterone leads him directly to genital sex—if not in reality, then at least in his own imagination.

Testosterone causes all of these physical changes in boys:

- Voice deepening
- Body hair growing
- Testicles dropping
- Sudden spurts in height
- Less vulnerable to fatigue, more single-minded
- More oxygen-carrying red blood cells bringing greater physical strength and endurance
- More sleep—an average of two hours more than before puberty

In the same way a girl's body is re-sculpted during puberty by estrogen, testosterone transforms a boy's body composition ratio to an average 40 percent lean mass and 15 percent fat.

Chemistry of Sports and Wet Dreams

If they dream about sex, teenage boys can wake up and discover they've ejaculated in their sleep, thus the "wet dream." With so much of their attention on sex, boys can easily become shy and embarrassed, imagining that others, particularly girls, can read their minds.

> **TURN-OFF**
>
> At this age, boys have so much testosterone in their bodies they can have an orgasm just from slow dancing with a girl or from a passing sexual thought with no help from anyone or anything else. It may be embarrassing, but it's totally normal.

Adolescent boys can become as moody as girls, spending hours each day in front of the mirror, obsessing about their appearance. Boys this age (and from here on) tend to talk less than girls, even less than they may have talked before puberty set in. In adolescence, most boys prefer nonverbal activities like video games and driving cars. Fortunately, boys can also work off their excess testosterone through sustained athletic activity.

A typical adolescent boy tends to act out his emotions physically rather than verbally. The aggression pathway in a young male's brain is tied to direct physical action, whereas a girl's is closely linked to cognitive and verbal functions.

Things That Can Mess with Puberty

Because of the number and scope of the biochemical changes that happen in adolescence, boys and girls have a much greater chance of getting derailed during these hyper-intense growth years. The vulnerabilities are greatest around the teen's self-image and blossoming sexuality. These first romantic relationships can set their expectations and patterns in love for a long time to come.

The two sources of a teen's most distressing emotions and irrational actions are these:

- Not being accepted by their same-sex friends

- Not being attractive or appealing to the opposite sex

Much of their worst behaviors are attempts to compensate for these fears and anxieties. Boys will display a notorious lack of judgment when it comes to their physical safety. Girls are especially susceptible to eating disorders and self-destructive behaviors like cutting. A large minority of adolescent boys and girls experiment with illegal drugs and alcohol to fit in and to cope with their own unruly emotions.

For parents, perspective, patience, and boundary-setting are vital if you and your teen are going to successfully make it through these years. Rational discussions with your teen may be difficult or impossible to have. Sometimes, asserting your authority in order to stop them from doing something dangerous is exactly what they need and want—not that they're likely to admit either. The best advice for the parent of a teenager: this too shall pass.

The Least You Need to Know

- With their immature neurons and oversized emotions, teens in love get the double whammy of dealing with their changing bodies *and* the volatile chemistry of romantic attraction—the same challenging rollercoaster at any age.

- Girls are more demonstrably moody and emotional than boys due to the newness of their hormonal fluctuations.

- Teen boys and girls crave touch, albeit different kinds.

Chemistry of Sexual Arousal and Orgasm

In This Chapter

- The chemicals essential for sex
- The science behind the hands-free orgasm
- The point of no return for a man's arousal
- Which hormone influences multiple orgasms

Sex is a four-phase process, neatly divided into the arousal, plateau, orgasm, and resolution phases. At the same time, each sexual experience is unique and slightly different from the one before and after. That's because neural and hormonal pathways are bi-directional, meaning the molecular messengers traveling on these routes can go in either direction. Sensory experiences make their way to the brain and become emotions. Your emotional state chemically changes how you experience the sights, sounds, smells, touch, and tastes of sexual passion. Meanwhile, the body's single-minded cast of chemical characters is doing its best to make sex pleasurable up to and including the ultimate "reward."

Arousal

The first stage of the sexual response cycle is arousal. It takes you from your first spark of desire through foreplay and intercourse to what's called "the plateau," which is the hottest you can get before reaching the "Big O." When the chemistry is right, it doesn't take much for arousal to take off. Thinking of her in a tight dress can make his pants a little, well, tighter. A whiff of his cologne as she opens the medicine chest can make her blush. If she gives him an affectionate pat on the behind, or he kisses her neck, the juices really get going.

Sexual feelings can be sparked by physically touching virtually any part of the human body: mouth, breast, foot, earlobe, and, of course, the genitals. But you can also be aroused without a physical stimulus. Researchers call this spontaneous or *cognitive arousal*. It can be prompted by a memory, a photo of your lover, an erotic film, even a thought. The chemistry of spontaneous arousal is the same as hands-on arousal. Start with higher testosterone, add liberal doses of dopamine, serotonin, and oxytocin courtesy of sexy thoughts and images, and you're there.

 DEFINITION

Cognitive arousal refers to the ability of men and women to experience sexual arousal, plateau, orgasm, and resolution without touching or being touched.

Eventually, the kisses and caresses of sexual foreplay include his and her genitals. When a woman fondles his penis and scrotum, and when a man strokes her clitoris and labia, nerve pulses from these areas travel by way of the central nervous system to the sensory-processing centers of the brain. When word reaches the hypothalamus (seat of the sex drive) and the amygdalae (mediating sexual arousal), they respond by triggering the release of the three chemicals without which there would be no pleasure from sex—and perhaps no sex at all.

Essential Chemicals in Arousal

In arousal, the three naturally occurring substances that lovers cannot live without are oxytocin, dopamine, and serotonin. They are secreted in response to signals of indirect (cognitive) and direct (sensory) stimulation. Once released, these three chemicals work in concert like a finely tuned orchestra.

Activated by estrogen and a player in every stage of sexual activity, oxytocin makes its showiest entrance into the bloodstream during arousal. It signals the circulatory system (heart and lungs) and sex organs to get into gear for full-tilt arousal. As these organs and systems go from static to active, more blood is pumped and breathing gets faster and deeper. In short order, the blood vessels and tissues around his penis and her clitoris receive more blood and become engorged or swollen.

Dopamine amplifies the flow of sensory impulses and literally turns on the brain's reward system. It stokes sex drive and increases the motivation to reach orgasm and every other kind of pleasure found in sex.

For men and women, serotonin increases responsiveness to sexual stimulation and enhances orgasm. In the plateau stage of arousal, serotonin interacts with dopamine to modulate a man's erection.

Other Hormones Involved in Arousal

Other hormones participate in the desire, arousal, and plateau stages of sex, although their exact roles and impact are not as clear. They affect both men and women.

Cortisol

Cortisol and certain related stress hormones are steroids secreted by the adrenal gland. It is thought that cortisol's impact is felt more as a suppressant on a man's sexual desire because higher levels of this hormone decrease his release of testosterone. This may also account for the psychological aspect of performance problems in men where stress, guilt, or other strong feelings can get in the way of his full participation in sex.

Prolactin

Synthesized by cells in the pituitary gland, prolactin can influence sexual response and orgasm. It is responsible for the feeling of sexual gratification after having sex, because it suppresses the effects of dopamine. When prolactin increases, it decreases dopamine and leads to the resolution period.

High levels of prolactin have been associated with diminished libido in men and in women, for whom high levels are naturally occurring during lactation. High levels of prolactin have also been tied to some neuroleptic drugs (tranquilizers used to treat psychotic conditions when a calming effect is desired) and antidepressants, especially the libido-depressing side effects of these drugs.

The Look and Feel of Arousal

So what does all this chemical activity look like on the outside? Several visible physical signs of arousal intensify as each of you gets closer to orgasm:

- Pupils dilate (especially in women)

- Blood pressure increases

- Heart rate doubles

- Pain threshold gets higher

Direct or indirect sexual stimulation can result in genital vasocongestion (engorgement) in both sexes. In women, sexual arousal often results in vaginal lubrication and an awareness of genital throbbing and tingling. In studies, not all women who experience these signs of sexual arousal say they feel subjectively aroused. Many women are not aware of physical sensations of sexual arousal, even when those body changes can be measured in the laboratory.

POINTER

Women are highly attuned to sounds in the background environment during intercourse and orgasm, while men are totally focused on the experience. This difference is thought to be instinctually hardwired into each sex, a vestige of a woman's role in monitoring any and all dangers to her young. It also explains why most men don't like to talk during sex (although before the plateau stage, especially if she talks "dirty" to him, seems to be fine).

How do researchers know this? One revealing tool is a vaginal probe with a light source and a light detector that measures changes in the amount of light reflected through the vaginal wall as an indication of changes in the amount of blood flow.

It goes without saying that for intercourse to occur, a man's penis must be erect and (ideally) a woman's vagina is expanded and lubricated to receive the penis. But how your chemistry produces this ideal state of affairs is a bit more complicated.

Intercourse

So, you may have long wondered, exactly how does he "get it up"? When dopamine produces a sharp increase in sensitivity to stimulation during the arousal stage, it helps activate a man's pelvic muscles and the blood vessels and tissues in his penis and scrotum. After that, there's only one way to go and that's up.

Dopamine facilitates erection and, eventually, ejaculation. Serotonin then acts as a brake to guard against too much dopamine, which can cause excessive relaxation, orgasm, and *premature ejaculation*.

DEFINITION

Premature ejaculation is a result of a dopamine rush and an emission of semen before the man wants it to occur. With emission, the penis becomes unengorged, which usually puts an end to intercourse. Affecting young men the most, a man can learn to control the timing of his orgasm and ejaculation.

No Stopping Now

Unlike a woman, there is a point during the plateau stage of arousal at which the man cannot stop the inevitability of his orgasm and ejaculation. That's because the nerve pulses to his pelvic muscles and the blood vessels of his genitals are already in the process of contracting, courtesy of the "brakes" of serotonin, in order to emit semen.

How Pain Becomes Pleasure

The relationship between pain and pleasure in sexual intercourse and other sexual activities has long been a subject of curiosity. We know that tolerance for pain goes up when people are sexually aroused. It appears that one part of the brain generates the emotion for pain. This emotion for pain is distinct from the physical feeling associated with a painful event. Still other brain neurons generate the pleasurable feelings of orgasm. But the signals for orgasmic pleasure and physical pain travel in very close pathways to the same location in the brain. Researchers think this could be part of the reason why the two experiences of pain and orgasmic pleasure overlap during sex.

SEXY FACT

Why is the anus sexually sensitive? Sensations from stimulation of the anus travel to the same part of the brain that receives sensations from the genitals. From there it's a short pathway to the brain's pleasure center.

Orgasm

The next major stage of sexual response after plateau is orgasm. Physically, an orgasm includes the involuntary contracting and releasing of the pelvic and anal muscles, with maximum tension and then relaxation lasting anywhere from 3 seconds up to a minute, with an average of 15 seconds.

However, because an orgasm is the culmination of a chemical, emotional, and physical process, it can be experienced in every part of the body. Your hands, feet, face, legs, and stomach may contract and relax along with your pelvis and sex organs. Blood can rush to all these areas carrying the hormones and neurotransmitters of pain or pleasure to receptors on many different organs and sites. Your skin can tingle, and the sum total of these body reactions can cause you to laugh and/or cry. Any and all emotions are possible; none is right or wrong.

The Brain and Orgasms

Brain scans have shown that an orgasm activates many areas of the brain but particularly the amygdalae (seat of the emotions) and the hippocampus (seat of short-term memory). It is thought that these brain centers work together to mediate (like a referee) the physical or visceral experience of orgasm with the cognitive and emotional dimensions. For comparison, brain scans taken of people watching an emotional film also show an activated amygdala.

What happens next varies from couple to couple. Unlike a man, once a woman's uterine and vaginal contractions of orgasm subside she can return immediately to the plateau or an earlier stage of arousal—another reason why she is capable of having multiple orgasms. And he's (usually) not.

Chemistry of Orgasms

Orgasms in men and women bring about the release of oxytocin, DHEA, prolactin, and endorphins. Some researchers believe that oxytocin may play a large role during and after orgasm. It may be involved in the man's sensory experience of his orgasm, and, along with endorphins, it may cause women to want to cuddle after they orgasm.

Release of oxytocin in women during intercourse has been connected to a man's sperm getting where it wants to go: to the woman's uterus. From animal studies, it's known that the release of oxytocin during orgasm acts to form strong affiliative or emotional bonds between two sex partners. It's not too much of a leap to think the same thing happens with humans.

Recent studies also show that prolactin is released in both men and women during orgasm. It is also thought to be responsible for the feeling of a hangover after particularly passionate sex. These results produced speculation that the prolactin released at orgasm almost immediately "feeds back" on the brain circuits related to sexual drive and inhibits desire. Prolactin gains access to certain spinal fluids from where it may impact key areas of the brain related to desire, such as the hypothalamus. This may explain why men rarely have multiple orgasms spaced close together, but doesn't seem to account for the ease with which some women do.

Are Orgasms Good for Your Health?

In ancient Egypt and Greece, the condition known as hysteria in women was thought to be a result of sexual deprivation. In the late nineteenth century, medical treatment of hysteria included the use of vibrators to assist women in achieving orgasm. Claims that orgasms bring about a general improvement in men's and women's health have existed for at least two millennia. In a British study done from 1979 to 1997, the frequency of orgasms in men was correlated with mortality rates. At the 10-year follow-up, researchers found that the mortality risk was 50 percent lower among men who had frequent orgasms, defined in this study as two or more per week.

Another research study in the late 1990s on middle-aged men pointed to a relationship between the levels of DHEA, which is released into the bloodstream at orgasm, and a reduction in the rate of heart disease.

For women, a correlation has been made between increased frequency of orgasms and less likelihood of developing endometriosis, an abnormality of the uterine tissue. And in perhaps the most surprising finding, researchers who interviewed nearly 2,000 pregnant women about their sex practices found that women who experienced orgasms throughout the three trimesters were more likely to carry their pregnancies to term.

Basking in the Afterglow

The fourth and final stage of the sexual response cycle is resolution, when your body returns to its pre-arousal state. The "bonus" blasts of oxytocin, endorphins, and dopamine that men and women receive with orgasm account for the peaceful, luminescent afterglow that often follows.

The Least You Need to Know

- Dopamine and serotonin work together to help a man get and keep his erection.
- Neighboring chemical and neural pathways account for the mingling of pain and pleasure in sex.
- Numerous studies have shown that the more orgasms a person has, the healthier he or she will be.
- A woman can restart her chemistry of arousal immediately after reaching orgasm.

Female Sexual Response

In This Chapter

- Why sexual desire in women is not essential for good sex
- How testosterone runs the show behind the scenes for women's libido
- The most common female sexual problems
- Treatments for low libido and difficulties with arousal and orgasms

The differences between men and women around sex begin with their reasons for doing it, and continue with what they like to do immediately afterward. The science of sexology has gathered the data to show what you may have already guessed on your own. Women's sexuality is highly contextual, meaning it has as much or more to do with the relationship and her emotional needs than the sex itself. How this plays out in a woman's body, and the chemical underpinnings of her sexual response, are the subject of this chapter.

Female Sexual Desire

When thinking about the chemistry of female arousal, it's important to distinguish between a woman's *sexual desire* and her response to arousal. The former helps stoke the latter, but it's not essential. This is something that hasn't always been understood, resulting in far too many stand-offs between horny men and ostensibly disinterested women across the land.

DEFINITION

Sexual desire is defined as having sexual thoughts, fantasies, dreams, or wishes—*before* a sexual interaction begins.

Here's a surprise. Sexual desire by itself is an uncommon reason for women to initiate sex or for a woman to agree to sexual activity. Women have sex for many other reasons before desire: to make an emotional connection, to please a partner, even to avoid a spat. Meanwhile, men, at least until they reach their forties, are walking around with a seemingly inexhaustible supply of sexual desire.

Fortunately, the chemistry of love has you covered in most eventualities. Here's the scoop, supported by the latest research. Even if sex is the furthest thing from her mind before he touches her, his actions can get her aroused and then launch their combined sexual chemistry, no matter whose idea it was at the start.

Getting in the Mood

A woman's level of sexual desire can vary for different reasons. The stage of her menstrual cycle, whether she's under stress, or if she's nursing a baby are all factors that can put the kibosh on how much she wants to do it tonight.

From a chemical perspective, her sex drive depends on there being higher levels of testosterone and estrogen in her system. A woman makes testosterone in her adrenal glands. Most women have far less of it than the average man, although about one third of women have the same or more testosterone than most men. In every case, testosterone plays a key role in creating and maintaining a woman's sex drive. The bottom line: research has established that women with more testosterone in their systems have more sex, and experience more orgasms.

SEXY FACT

Although the surgical removal of a woman's ovaries (producing estrogen) reduces sexual desire somewhat, the removal of her adrenal glands (producing testosterone) has an even stronger dampening effect on a woman's desire for sex.

Recent studies are coming up with some other fascinating tidbits about women and testosterone. It turns out that a woman's testosterone level increases when she's in her male lover's presence, and decreases in his absence. Some researchers tie these fluctuations to the effects of the man's pheromone on the woman's endocrine system; it may be what's cueing her to produce more testosterone.

Sexologists Lisa Dawn Hamilton and Cindy Meston at the University of Texas in Austin did a study looking into this phenomenon. They found that the amount of testosterone measured in the saliva of 15 female participants (all of whom were involved in long-distance relationships where they saw their partners once a month on average) was lowest when these women were apart from their partners for at least two weeks. The women were then retested before and after being reunited with their boyfriends. Interestingly, they found that testosterone levels were highest in these women on the day *before* their partner's return, and then again on the day after the couple had renewed sexual activity. Sounds like the brain's anticipatory reward system working overtime!

Getting from Zero to Sixty

Sexual arousal in either sex is defined in terms that are both subjective (feeling sexually excited) and physiological (genitals engorged). A woman's sexual arousal, meaning everything that she feels and experiences physically after she and her partner start foreplay, is primarily a product of the release of oxytocin and dopamine in her brain. These are the chemicals secreted by the hypothalamus and pituitary, which enter her bloodstream in response to stimuli; e.g., the smell of her lover's sweat, or his mouth on her breast.

It also helps a woman to become aroused if her progesterone level is low, as it is during the first half of her menstrual period. Progesterone, highest in weeks three and four of the menstrual period, produces a sedating effect. It also decreases a woman's uterine sensitivity to oxytocin, thus dampening her sex drive while blunting her orgasmic response.

Estrogen, which increases during the first two weeks of her menstrual cycle and then rapidly decreases, makes a woman more sexually receptive. It also increases vaginal lubrication to enable penetration in intercourse.

Female Arousal Response

Most women get aroused from stimulation of their nipples, cervix, clitoris, and vagina. Nerve endings in each of these areas of her body trigger the female brain to release oxytocin. Among a seemingly endless list of positive effects, oxytocin in the plateau stage of sexual arousal causes the expansion of a woman's vaginal muscles in preparation for the man's penis.

It is thought that the combination of oxytocin and estrogen pushes a woman to experience the desire for vaginal penetration. This urge, sometimes described by women as a desire "to be filled up," is probably connected to the female's evolutionary drive to become pregnant and move her genes, and those of her lover, into future generations.

Pain and Pleasure

Breast or nipple stimulation can be enough to bring some women to orgasm without any other form of direct stimulation. How is that? The orgasm-inducing effect of breast stimulation may be due to sensory nerve pulses from the breasts and genitals traveling to the same group of neurons in the brain's reward circuit. When these neurons are stimulated, they signal the secretion of more oxytocin and dopamine.

Here's one more helpful contribution to a woman's sexual experience, courtesy of oxytocin. During sexual intercourse, because of this hormone, her response to pain is half its normal level. Meanwhile, her sensitivity to touch, again due to high oxytocin, is greater.

It should also be noted that pain during intercourse is a common female sexual issue that should not be ignored. If the use of lubricants does not help reduce or eliminate the problem, a doctor should be consulted to check for other possible problems.

The Distracted Female

One major difference between men's and women's sexual response has to do with a woman's greater susceptibility to fears and anxieties that can distract her from sexual arousal.

TURN-OFF

Unlike a man, a woman can lose interest in sex at any moment up to and including orgasm. For a woman to stay turned on, the fear-worry circuit in her brain must be turned off.

How does fear or worry cause a woman to turn off sexually? Negative feelings such as fear and anxiety are modulated in the amygdala. When activated, the amygdalae sends its chemical messengers to the frontal cortex. If emotional distractions flare up for a woman during any point in the arousal stage, the announcement goes out loud and clear from her brain to the rest of her body: "forget sex."

If the woman is free of such negative thoughts and feelings, and she has received sufficient stimulation of her clitoris and/or vagina, she is free to reach the Big O. The experience is physical, emotional, and often ecstatic, even spiritual for many women. Not all orgasms are the same, even for the same woman. Most include some combination of involuntary rhythmic pelvic, uterine, and anal contractions, along with peak sensations of pleasure and a warm and fuzzy sense of contentment.

The Female Orgasm

Women's orgasms have been studied by scientists for decades, with a sense of mystery still surrounding the subject. This most likely has to do with the lack of precise understanding of what happens in a woman's brain when she reaches sexual climax. It's also often noted that unlike the male orgasm, the female "Big O" is not essential for reproduction, although researchers suggest that women's orgasms increase the probability of conception.

Aspects of the experience of a woman reaching orgasm can be broken down as either biological or psychological. Combining these perspectives, a team of researchers including Cindy Meston came up with the following definition (minus a few technical terms):

> *An orgasm in the human female is a variable, transient peak sensation of intense pleasure, creating an altered state of conscious-ness, usually with an initiation accompanied by the involuntary rhythmic contractions of the muscles of the pelvis often with uterine and anal contractions, and a slow relaxation of the muscles that resolves the sexually induced engorgement generally with an induc-tion of well-being and contentment.*

Phew! Got that?

Two Types of Female Orgasms

A comparative difference between men's and women's orgasms, pointed out in the paper by Meston and her colleagues, is that only women's orgasms are broken down into different types. There's a fair amount of confusion among women about this topic, but to put it simply, clitoral orgasms are achieved by direct stimulation of the clitoris, while the vaginal or coital variety occur during intercourse. When women in research studies were asked to describe the different experiences they had with each type of orgasm, here were some of their self-reported descriptions:

- Clitoral orgasms were described as warm, ticklish, electrical, and sharp.

- Vaginal orgasms were said to produce sensations that are throbbing, deep, soothing, and comfortable.

When the pioneer sex researchers Masters and Johnson first exam-ined the female orgasm back in the 1960s, they reached the con-clusion that both the clitoral and vaginal orgasm were, from a physiological perspective, one and the same experience. More recent laboratory-based research has established a scientific basis for differ-ences between the two. They are thought to be caused by distinct patterns of uterine (smooth, involuntary muscle) and pelvic muscular activity associated with each type. It's also fair to say that many female orgasms involve both clitoral and vaginal stimulation and response.

Comparing Men's and Women's Orgasms

Although the psychological and emotional experiences of orgasm tend to be described similarly by the two sexes, men and women have some other important physiological differences:

- Unlike most males, females can have repeated (multiple) orgasms separated by short intervals of time, although some men can have repeated orgasms but not ejaculate; once they ejaculate, they need a recovery period.

- Females can have orgasms of longer duration.

- Women's orgasms can be interrupted "mid-stream," but men's cannot be stopped after they begin.

Taken as a whole, the pleasurable gender-linked advantages appear to be spread equally between males and females.

Female Post-Orgasm Reaction

For the woman, post orgasm, a major source of contentment comes from a powerful and voluminous release of oxytocin. This hormonal flood arrives approximately one minute after a woman's orgasm, but can stay in her blood for up to five minutes. Its emotional effects can last much longer.

Roadblocks to Female Sexual Pleasure

According to an article in the *Journal of the American Medical Association*, as many as 43 percent of women have some form of difficulty in their sexual function, compared to 31 percent of men. A recent article in the *Journal of Urology* defined female sexual dysfunction (FSD) as including such varied troubles as a lack of sexual desire so great that it causes personal distress, an inability of the genitals to become adequately lubricated, difficulty in reaching orgasm even after sustained stimulation, and a persistent genital pain associated with intercourse.

Female Low Libido

The number one reported sexual problem of women is low libido (desire). Low libido in pre-menopausal women has a variety of causes. Some are physical, others are psychological, and many involve both. The exact number of women affected varies greatly, but a consistently large minority of women in popular and scientific surveys consistently say they experience a lack of sexual desire. It's not always clear whether the woman responding to these surveys is the one who believes her low libido is "a problem," or whether the woman's sex partner has characterized her lack of desire that way.

Problems with low libido and inhibited orgasms affect women in every age group. The physical causes of female sexual dysfunction can range from having too little testosterone or estrogen in the blood, to severed nerves as a result of pelvic surgery, to taking such medications as antihistamines or certain antidepressants. The psychological factors can include sexual history issues, relationship problems, and depression.

Testosterone treatment of some women with low sexual desire has been shown to be somewhat effective. However, close monitoring is important to guard against cardiovascular effects and unwanted body and skin changes, including hair growth.

Problems Getting Aroused

Some women experience difficulties becoming aroused in response to any form of direct stimulation. In studies, this problem has been measured by examining physiological indications of vasocongestion (swelling of the vulva, clitoris) and vaginal lubrication, which are lower in women with this now-medically recognized clinical dysfunction. Many women who suffer from it say they can still feel subjectively aroused by viewing an erotic film, being kissed, or receiving breast stimulation. But they complain of minimal genital response, including a lack of orgasms.

Women who have been diagnosed with different versions of this problem include those with autonomic nerve damage; an estrogen deficiency, which allows for sexual sensations from vulval stimulation but insufficient lubrication for intercourse; menopausal women (who naturally have lower estrogen) with no genital response; and the most common version of the complaint, a woman with an inability to experience either genital or subjective arousal response.

It should be noted that not all women react to their low sexual response with distress. In fact, the scale of reactions typically ranges from none to severe distress. What works for a particular woman varies depending on her age, relationship status, and other lifestyle or health issues. Sexologists who treat women for sexual problems suggest the following issues be considered when diagnosing and treating women for their sexual concerns:

- Psychosocial factors such as negative upbringing, losses, trauma, and cultural/religious restrictions

- Current relationship issues, partner sexual dysfunctions, inadequate sexual stimulation, unsatisfactory emotional and sexual contexts

- Medical and mental health conditions, medications, or substance abuse

Again, such a list of factors supports the observation that a woman's sexuality is often highly contextual.

Problems Reaching Orgasm

Although all females have the physical ability to experience orgasm, in one survey of 1,749 randomly selected American women, 24 percent of those responding reported no orgasmic function within the last seven months or more.

Of course, not all women routinely have orgasms during intercourse; some surveys put the numbers who do at less than 20 percent. The majority of women need direct clitoral stimulation during early arousal and/or during intercourse. Communication between sex partners and experimentation with positions and arousal techniques can enhance a woman's ability to reach orgasm.

For the 7 to 10 percent of *anorgasmic* women who say they never experience orgasms either during sex or through masturbation, treatments involve psychotherapy and behavioral modification. A psychotherapist seeks to help the woman reduce her anxiety and reframe any negative thoughts she may have to give her a more positive attitude about her sexuality. Behavioral techniques include directed masturbation and Kegel muscle exercises. To date, no medications have been shown to be effective for treating anorgasmia in women.

> **DEFINITION**
>
> The medical term for a woman's (or man's) problems in reaching orgasm is **anorgasmia.**

Directed masturbation is the most frequently prescribed treatment for anorgasmic women. The successive stages of directed masturbation train a woman to locate and manually stimulate genital areas that bring her sexual pleasure. The process often begins with the woman making a visual exploration of her body using a mirror and visual information on female anatomy. Once she learns how to achieve orgasm alone, her partner is introduced into the directed masturbation sessions. With the man's inclusion, the woman gradually loses the anxiety she had regarding sexual stimulation, and the partner learns how to better stimulate her.

Drugs with Sexual Side Effects for Women

Certain oral contraceptives that increase progesterone throughout the female cycle have been associated with decreased sexual interest and libido in women taking them.

Some studies indicate that patients prescribed selective serotonin reuptake inhibitors, referring to the SSRI class of antidepressant medications including Prozac, Paxil, and the SNRI Effexor, report sexual side effects from these medications. Problems reported include low libido and an inability to reach orgasm.

Newer antidepressant medications that act by increasing levels of dopamine and norepinephrine, including Bupropion (brand name Wellbutrin), have shown fewer side effects. In some studies they've been shown to increase libido and the frequency of orgasms in women.

Some over-the-counter drugs can have unwanted sexual side effects on women. For example, antihistamines can cause vaginal dryness.

The Least You Need to Know

- A woman can and often does become aroused only after the man initiates sex.
- Fears and anxiety in women can kill arousal at any point during sex.
- Although oxytocin is essential for the arousal stage of men and women, women have a much higher tolerance for its cuddling effects after orgasm.
- There are effective behavioral and psychological therapies for the up to 24 percent of women who experience problems reaching an orgasm.

Male Sexual Response

In This Chapter

- The skinny on how to measure a penis
- How the brain controls the stages of a man's sexual experience from his initial surge of desire to orgasm
- How oxytocin makes him nod off after orgasms
- How medications for erectile dysfunction work

There is a mistaken impression out there that male sexuality is simple, the course of a man's arousal and sexual satisfaction a no-brainer, and the changes over his life cycle minimal. Partly this has to do with the fact that male genitalia are external, and thus are more easily understood (and aroused).

But as any man and any couple is aware, there are moods and seeming mysteries attached to men's sexuality, too. There are times when a man in his thirties and forties cannot achieve an erection and he doesn't have a clue why he can't. There are times when stress feeds his sexual desire and still others when disappointment over some perceived failure in his life kills all thoughts of sex. Could it be that a man's emotions have more to do with his sexual performance than he thought? This would put a dent in the "man as sex machine" theory—and that might not be a bad thing.

As this chapter shows, male sexual desire and response, as well as his roadblocks to pleasure, have a biochemical and emotional basis and are highly dependent on what else is going on in his body and mind.

The Penis: A User's Guide

Let's begin with the obvious issue of size. Determining the average penis size for a group of males, let alone for men around the world, is more complicated than you might imagine. Unfortunately most information about average penis size comes from popular culture and not science. Let's start by considering some figures from science.

The results from three studies of penis size, where the measurements were taken in a laboratory setting, give the following ranges:

- Average penis length (flaccid/not erect): from 3.4 inches to 3.7 inches (8.6 cm to 9.3 cm)

- Average penis length (erect): from 5.1 inches to 5.7 inches (12.9 cm to 14.5 cm)

- Average penis girth (circumference when erect, averaged from base, middle, and just below the tip): from 3.5 inches to 3.9 inches (8.8 cm to 10 cm)

These numbers are obviously very different from the sizes seen in adult movies and heard about in barroom conversations. Many, possibly most, statistics you read are not from legitimate research but from marketing companies who want men to feel bad about their penis size so as to encourage them to buy a dubious product designed to lengthen it.

So here are some facts about penis size:

- There is much greater variation in size of flaccid (nonerect) penises than of penises when they are erect. A soft penis that looks large may be roughly the same size when erect as a soft penis that looks smaller.

- Because most men see other penises when they are not erect, it can appear as if there is a big difference, and men may assume their erect penis is much smaller when compared to others.

There's more about the anatomy and operation of the penis during erection and orgasm later in this chapter.

Male Sexual Desire

Testosterone is the primary chemical setting a man's sexual agenda. Although it doesn't directly affect a man's erection (except to increase his sexual desire), testosterone in his system makes him single-minded until he copulates with his sexual partner.

When it's time for the man to enter the woman, dopamine aids penile erection and ejaculation by intensifying neural stimulation during the final stage of arousal. When serotonin puts the brakes on his dopamine surge so as to avoid premature ejaculation, the action is called a "tonic inhibition." In other words, it delivers not too much or too little, but just the right amount of dopamine so he can hold his erection for as long as needed.

Male Arousal Response

Similar to women, stimulation of a man's genitals in arousal triggers the release of oxytocin in the pleasure/reward circuit of his brain. In men, oxytocin acts as a neurotransmitter (not in its usual role as a hormone in the bloodstream) traveling down the nerve fibers next to the spinal cord to his pelvic area. With the help of dopamine, the nerves extending from the base of the spinal cord and running to the end of his penis cause the smooth muscles of his penis to relax, not unlike the effect of fingers loosening their grip on a hose.

As *vasocongestion* takes place, the spongy erectile tissue and the many blood vessels of the man's penis will enlarge to their maximum capacity. A pair of nerves (pudenal) in the penis then contracts, and intensifies his erection.

DEFINITION

Vasocongestion is the filling of tissues and organs (in men and women) with blood. This swelling happens to the penis, labia, and clitoris during sexual arousal, causing erections in these areas.

Blood flow to the penis temporarily ceases during erection. After a man ejaculates, blood exits his penis and the nerves and muscles go back to stasis. The penis returns to its normal flaccid state.

Male Orgasm

As it does for women, a man's brain has everything to do with his orgasm. A greater area of his brain is dedicated to the nerve endings and processing of sexual signals. If sensory impulses from penile stimulation don't reach the brain, such as when there's been a spinal cord injury, the man doesn't experience the pleasure of arousal or orgasm.

Although many people think a man's orgasm is the same as his ejaculation, it is not. Even though the two usually occur at the same time, they don't have to. A man can have an orgasm without ejaculating. In this case, the semen goes backward toward his bladder, rather than out the urethra. This is called retrograde ejaculation.

Premature Ejaculation

Another myth of male sexuality would have men consider premature ejaculation as a disease. Premature ejaculation does exist as a clinical diagnosis, but it's not a disease or illness.

The *Diagnostic and Statistical Manual of Mental Disorders, Fourth Edition (DSM-IV-TR)*, emphasizes "persistent and recurrent ejaculation with minimal sexual stimulation before, on, or shortly after penetration before the person wishes it," and "marked distress or interpersonal difficulty" as its criteria for a diagnosis of premature ejaculation.

This is a subject replete with myths and misunderstandings. The causes of premature ejaculation are still unknown, but it's most often considered to be the consequence of psychological rather than physical issues. Some men believe that if they put their attention elsewhere during sex, and not on their own bodies, "it" will work better. This, however, is not true.

TURN-OFF

The best chance a man has of controlling ejaculation is to pay *more* attention to his body, not less. The "distraction" method may work for some people, some of the time, but it isn't a solution, because it takes the man away from experiencing sexual pleasure.

Most men can learn to both experience full sexual pleasure and control ejaculation—it just takes practice. No one is born with the ability to control ejaculation. It seems likely that early masturbatory experiences and sexual experiences with partners may play a role in what a man's sexual response is like, and how aware he is of ejaculatory control, but ejaculation is an automatic response like urination: the only way to control it is to learn how.

Another misconception is that if you ejaculate within a few minutes, you're a premature ejaculator. Some definitions of premature ejaculation include a specific time limit but many do not. The definitions that indicate a time limit usually also require other symptoms for premature ejaculation to be diagnosed.

Premature ejaculation may be the most common male sexual dysfunction, particularly for men under the age of 40. According to the National Health and Social Life Survey (NHSLS) 30 percent of men across all adult age categories live with premature ejaculation, but very few men ever talk about it.

Finally, premature ejaculation is a problem that can be treated. There are several very successful ways of treating premature ejaculation. In most cases men can learn to control ejaculation without drugs or medical intervention. Behavioral methods to treat premature ejaculation are very effective. They also have the benefits of increasing a man's understanding of his own sexual response, and of increasing sexual communication with his partner. There are currently no FDA-approved medications to treat premature ejaculation.

Male Post-Orgasm Reaction

By the time men reach orgasm, they have accumulated three to five times their usual amount of oxytocin. Both the duration and effects of this hormone are different for men and women after orgasm.

Post-orgasmic oxytocin gives a woman an even greater sensitivity to touch and a desire for more physical contact. At this stage most women want to cuddle. Estrogen works with oxytocin to reduce stress hormones, leaving her feeling relaxed and content. If he's ready, she can often go for another round of intercourse.

Meanwhile, men don't ordinarily retain as much oxytocin in their systems, and what they receive at orgasm goes away faster. This gives him far less interest in a big post-orgasmic cuddle. Testosterone also makes men less able to enjoy the stress-relieving effects of oxytocin, as compared with women. On top of that, because men are not as accustomed to oxytocin, it is thought they become "drunk" from the sudden flush they receive with orgasm.

This makes men sluggish, a brain state that can be measured as "theta," the same state associated with nursing women (who are also under the heavy influence of oxytocin). When men receive their extra wallop of oxytocin with an orgasm, a common reaction is to fall asleep … much to the chagrin of women, who find themselves wide awake and ready to chat after reaching orgasm.

Roadblocks to Male Sexual Pleasure

Testosterone affects a man's temperament in many ways beyond his sex drive. For example, normally cycling low testosterone can reduce a man's energy level and his competitive urge. Similarly, when negative life experiences such as a job loss deflate a man's ego and depress his emotional health, his sex drive and sexual performance can also be hindered.

Stress on the job or elsewhere in a man's life can have a positive or negative effect on his sexuality, depending on his habitual response to such factors. However, if the stress causes the release of too much of the stress hormone cortisol in his body, it can have an inhibitory affect on a man's sexual performance.

Male Low Libido

Male testosterone levels decrease naturally with age, bringing libido down gradually from its height in a man's late teens and twenties. Testosterone levels drop off for a man as a natural consequence of his aging. It happens first and only slightly in his thirties and forties, and more in his fifties and sixties. Some refer to this later cycle in a

man's life when his testosterone is at its lowest level as male menopause or andropause.

A man's libido may drop in earlier periods of his life for different
reasons. There is a potential chain reaction between a man's professional failure, or his perception of himself as a failure, and a drop in
his testosterone level. This lower testosterone (lower than what it was
before) then reduces his sex drive.

Testosterone Treatment for Low Libido

Testosterone therapy for low sexual desire is given to men who have
measurably low levels of the sex hormone in their system. For such
men, supplements of testosterone can have a tonic effect, including
restoring sex drive and aiding erection, orgasm, and ejaculation.
There is some thought that restoring testosterone to a man whose
level has dropped can also function as an antidepressant. It should be
noted that if a man's testosterone level is normal and he receives extra
testosterone, there are likely to be none of these positive effects.

POINTER

As they age, men (like women at any age) need more time to become
sexually aroused than they did when they were younger. More time kissing and cuddling will help men achieve equally satisfying erections and
orgasms; he will just get there differently.

Testosterone supplements (known as testosterone replacement
therapy or TRT) can be delivered orally, using a patch, implanting a
pellet, or through injections. The benefits of TRT must be carefully
weighed against its potential to speed the growth of prostate cancer,
which is relatively common in men as they age. Other side effects
of testosterone supplements can include salt and water retention, a
problem for those with hypertension.

Always discuss the pros and cons of any hormonal treatments with
your doctor.

Male Performance Problems

It's very common for a man of any age to have a problem achieving an erection once in a while. Reasons include exhaustion, stress, guilt, obesity, illness, medications, excessive alcohol intake, and drug abuse. In Chapter 14, we go into detail on the chemical basis for the interference of these and other voluntary or controllable factors with male sexuality.

Erectile dysfunction, also called ED, typically develops beginning in a man's forties (although it also happens to men in their twenties and thirties), with the likelihood increasing in each decade thereafter. When erections are chronically difficult or absent, a condition referred to as impotence, the reason could be a more serious physical or medical cause, for example, cardiovascular disease or nerve damage resulting from either diabetes or prostate cancer. Or the problem could stem from a chemical reaction with a prescription medication for blood pressure or depression. These and other medicines are known to interfere with male sex hormones or the neurotransmitters involved in his sexual arousal, such as dopamine or serotonin.

In older men, ED usually has a physical cause, such as disease, injury, or medication side effects. Incidence increases with age: about 5 percent of 40-year-old men and between 15 and 25 percent of 65-year-old men experience ED.

How ED Medications Work

The normal sequence of events in a man's erection impacted by ED medications can be summarized as follows:

- The parasympathetic nerves that stimulate the penis into an erection are influenced by the release of two chemicals called "first messengers," nitric oxide (NO) and acetylcholine (a regulator of involuntary or smooth muscles).

- These chemicals influence the release of relaxing factors in the cells that form the lining of the blood vessels in the penis.

- The combined effect is to relax the smooth (involuntary) muscles of the column of erectile tissue known as the *corpora cavernosa*, allowing increased blood flow to the penis and making it rigid.

- So-called "second messengers," cyclic nucleotides, are released, causing relaxation of the blood vessels and erectile tissue.

DEFINITION

Corpora cavernosa are a pair of spongelike, rod-shaped tissues along the length of the penis containing "sinuses" that become engorged with blood, resulting in an erection.

Erection is normally short-lived because an enzyme in the penis, phosphodiesterase-5, breaks down the cyclic nucleotides, thereby deactivating them. Pharmacological blocking of this enzyme's actions then allows them to prolong the smooth-muscle relaxation and hence the erection.

This is the mechanism of action of sildenafil and those chemically related erection enhancers known by the trade names Viagra, Cialis, and Levitra.

Use of ED Medications

Medications to treat erectile dysfunction debuted in the late 1990s and have grown in popularity ever since. An interesting side note to these drugs is that their discovery came about unexpectedly as a result of research and development of a drug for the treatment of cardiac-related pain and blood vessel constriction in the chest.

An article published in the *International Journal of Impotence Research* reported that from 1998 to 2002, prescriptions of Viagra had gone up 312 percent. Apparently, the major increase in its use was not among men over 50. Rather, it was for men between the ages of 18 and 45, suggesting that the motivation for its use was to increase the duration of erections in these younger men, not as a response to erectile dysfunction.

Drugs with Sexual Side Effects in Men

As they do in women, the SSRI class of antidepressants, including those with the trade names Prozac and Paxil, can cause sexual side effects in men. Antidepressants that increase dopamine and norepinephrine (e.g., Wellbutrin) have fewer reported negative effects, and may have positive effects on both sexual desire and erectile function in both sexes.

Many drugs that control high blood pressure, including commonly prescribed diuretics and beta-blockers, produce sexual problems in men and women. They can cause erectile dysfunction in men, and when taken by women, they can diminish sexual desire.

Finally, some nonprescription medications can negatively affect sex drive or performance. For example, antihistamines can cause erectile dysfunction or ejaculation problems in men.

The Least You Need to Know

- A penis that looks the same size as another man's when erect can be a very different size when flaccid.
- Thirty percent of men deal with premature ejaculation, which can best be treated with behavioral methods.
- Low male libido is successfully treated with testosterone supplements.
- Some stress can enhance a man's desire. Too much stress can inhibit his sexual performance.

Women's Cycles, Men's Cycles

Chapter 12

In This Chapter

- Which days of the month women are likely to be most receptive to sex
- The time of day men are most and least horny
- Which two neurochemicals that dictate who's in charge and when

Traditionally, a woman's blue or irritable moods are blamed on her hormones acting up at certain times of the month. In fact, some 15 to 20 percent of women describe the cramps, bloating, tension, lethargy, headaches, and depressed feelings they experience before a period as severe, while another 30 percent describe their premenstrual symptoms as moderately bothersome.

But how often do you hear about a man's hormone cycle affecting his state of mind or mood? Well, men's bodies change in predictable, hormone-orchestrated patterns, too. Actually, adult-male testosterone levels shift many times every day. Meanwhile, up to six hormones are fluctuating at any given point in the month for a pre-menopausal female. So while a woman's chemicals are lining up to give pregnancy a chance, her sex drive and arousal responses must tag along for the ride. And wherever her hormones go, his must follow. Or so it's always been assumed. In this chapter, we find out where the two of you are headed, and when you have the best chances of meeting up along the way.

Women's Monthly Cycle

It starts with her first menstrual period in puberty. The cycles take a while to become stable, and there remains considerable range in cycle length. Most adult women have cycles from about 21 days to 35 days in length, and medical textbooks use a 28-day cycle as their model. The menstrual cycle is best thought of as two halves, with radically different hormones pushing her body and moods in at least two very different directions. Each stage of her cycle can and often does show up in her level of sexual desire and response to arousal.

To summarize, in the first half of a 28-day cycle, her hypothalamus releases a substance called gonadotrophin releasing hormone (GnRH). This hormone then acts on the anterior pituitary and causes it to release two substances, follicle-stimulating hormone (FSH) and luteinizing hormone (LH). These substances then activate the ovaries and cause them to release estrogen. Estrogen flows throughout the body, including back to the hypothalamus, creating a feedback loop. At some point, the presence of estrogen signals the hypothalamus to stop producing GnRH, and the anterior pituitary decreases its production of FSH and LH. This results in an overall drop of estrogen in the woman's body.

By the midpoint of her cycle, estrogen has increased dramatically and softens her emotions, and makes her generally more sexually receptive. This flow of estrogen reaches its peak when a woman ovulates. She then releases an egg from an ovary, making this midpoint her most fertile time of the month.

Coinciding with her high estrogen, oxytocin and endorphins in a woman's system make her sensory nerves—the nerve endings of her skin, genitals, lips, and just about everywhere else on her body—more sensitive.

POINTER

Men, know your lady's cycle. Many women have more sexual desire when they are ovulating, halfway through their cycle.

One study done at Emory University found that women spent more time looking at sexually explicit photos when they had the most estrogen in their system during their menstrual cycle. This peak occurs at the midpoint of a woman's 28-day cycle and coincides with ovulation.

After ovulation, sexual responsiveness changes like day turns to night. In the third and fourth weeks of each monthly cycle, estrogen rapidly decreases and progesterone replaces estrogen as the dominant hormonal player. Added to this progesterone surge is the lactation hormone prolactin, another sex cooler. By the time we factor in the sobering influences of vasopressin and serotonin, you've got a woman who is much more likely to want to be left alone.

As week four arrives, progesterone makes a final dramatic drop to trigger a pre-menopausal woman's menstrual bleeding. This exit of progesterone leaves the woman's testosterone, estrogen, and endorphins behind to essentially direct her sexual desire and response.

Cycle of Female Sexual Response

What man hasn't noticed the difference a week or two can make in his lady's sex drive? How many women have wondered if they've suddenly lost romantic interest in the man they were sexually hungry for just a few days ago? Let's explore the chemical logic behind this apparent irrationality before it wreaks havoc with your sex life.

Looking again at weeks one and two in a woman's monthly menstrual cycle, we find estrogen everywhere in her body. The word most often used to describe this stage in a woman's sexual ebb and flow is "receptive." If this generality were to hold true and you were casting a French film in the first half of a woman's menstrual cycle, you'd hire the sex kitten (as opposed to the tiger).

At the end of the second week, midpoint in her cycle when a woman ovulates, most women have an increase in their sexual desire and interest in intercourse. It is thought that the higher level of estrogen and testosterone in her system at this time makes her more receptive to intercourse at this midpoint in her cycle—compared to other times in her cycle when she's simply feeling hot or cold toward sex.

Men, I hope you caught that window, because it only lasts two or three days and it's about to close. Right after ovulation, progesterone, vasopressin, serotonin, and prolactin will have the combined effect of inhibiting her sex drive and dampening her arousal response. Another impact of this gang of four chemicals is to increase a woman's mental clarity. And if clear thought leads her to think twice about sex, well, men, just wait another week, and you'll have reason to try again.

Right before she menstruates—and for some women even while they're bleeding—a woman's sexual desire often rebounds. With progesterone no longer blocking the neural receptors in her body for testosterone, testosterone is free to act up again.

You may be surprised to hear of some women's heightened sex drive so near to menstruation, prime time for premenstrual bloating, tension, and cramps. Still, many women report that the week before their periods is when they describe themselves as feeling most horny. It's possible that sex relieves some of the stress and tension of a woman's premenstrual syndrome.

Hormones and Pregnancy

A woman's orgasm, following that of her mate, is thought to assist her in becoming pregnant. That's because the muscle contractions of orgasm, primarily those of the cervix, aid the man's sperm in its quest to fertilize the woman's egg and implant in her uterus.

Conception occurs when the woman's egg travels down the fallopian tube of the ovary and is greeted by millions of sperm. One sperm will manage to locate the receptor site, allowing it to break through the protective coating on the egg, and then burrow inside. This action signals to the other sperm that conception has occurred, and the cells begin to multiply. Some cells will become the embryo, while others will become the placenta, the amniotic sac that surrounds the baby, or the umbilical cord. At this point, the structure is free-floating, and needs to implant itself on the wall of the womb.

Implantation usually takes several days. The fertilized egg implants in the mother's uterine lining and attaches to her blood supply. The developing embryo releases a chemical that tells the mother's body to produce progesterone, which thickens the uterine lining and stops the woman from menstruating. The constant high levels of progesterone gives her a sedated feeling. The woman's brain is then exposed to all the hormones manufactured by her fetus and its placenta. Estrogen stays high and plays an important role in providing proper circulation to the developing fetus. A spike in the manufacturing of her stress hormones does not necessarily produce anxiety but has the effect of putting her total focus on the well-being of the baby developing inside her. Not since puberty have so many hormonal changes gone on in a woman as when she becomes pregnant.

For many women, this state of hormonal flux does not dampen sex drive. And regular sex also appears to be good for maintaining a healthy pregnancy. A review of 59 studies done between 1950 and 1996 concluded that sexual activity during pregnancy, even with the chemical and physical impact of arousal and intercourse, doesn't harm the fetus. In fact, preterm delivery was significantly reduced for women who had intercourse in the last trimester of pregnancy.

As any parent knows, if you're about to have a newborn in the house, you should enjoy any late-pregnancy sex while you can. After giving birth, a euphoric shower of oxytocin and dopamine produces what many call the "mommy brain." In this state, a mother only has eyes for her baby.

The Little-Known Male Cycle

Although the female monthly cycle involves multiple chemicals, and its links to a woman's changing moods are widely discussed, men have a little-known, even less understood sexual cycle of their own. It involves only one chemical—you guessed it: the male hormone, testosterone. One reason it is so poorly understood is because testosterone changes rapidly with one's environment and mood, so measuring it can be challenging.

- The male cycle occurs once every 24 hours, with peaks 6 or 7 times a day and smaller fluctuations occurring every 15 to 20 minutes.

- The range of testosterone levels in a man's blood is very broad.

- Testosterone levels also change with the seasons; in the mid-summer his level is highest, and it's lowest in winter and early spring. So much for all that talk of love budding with the blooms of spring!

- Testosterone levels in a man are generally highest in the morning and lowest at night.

A man's high testosterone level in the morning makes him most virile upon waking. This explains why men often wake up with an erection. Comparatively, he's got less desire at dusk, especially as he ages.

TURN-OFF

Studies have shown that men with the highest testosterone levels and the most handsome men are more likely to cheat on their partners and be divorced. Could this be evidence of too much of a good thing? Researchers say the evidence points to exactly that conclusion.

Sexual desire and testosterone levels are linked in an unending feedback loop in men. Testosterone is increased through his regular sexual activity, and high testosterone leads him to want and have more sex. In addition to increasing a man's sex drive, a higher level of testosterone is beneficial to a healthy heart and brain. It produces a buoyant effect on his mood and energy level.

The Serotonin Connection

It may be that a man's ascension to positions of power and importance is linked to fluctuations in his serotonin level. According to anthropologist Helen Fisher writing in *Anatomy of Love: A Natural History of Mating, Marriage, and Why We Stray*, the neurochemical serotonin has been shown to affect the status of the male of several mammal species, including humans.

In studies, monkeys of highest rank in a clan have the highest levels of this mood-elevating neurotransmitter. When serotonin is injected into lower-ranking monkeys, their rank jumped up. When a serotonin inhibitor is given to high-ranking monkeys, their status precipitously fell. Among college student groups, male officers show higher levels of serotonin in their blood than nonofficers. Interestingly, there was no such correlation between serotonin and female college students or female monkeys. Fisher suggests this gender difference reflects females' more complex and subtle system of ranking in groups.

The Cycle of Love Chemistry

Both men and women are subject to a much longer and, one might say, more profound cycle that controls the way we love over a lifetime. Teenagers fall in love to practice the rituals of courtship. Romantic love as experienced in one's twenties and early thirties is a process of weeding out the strongest potential mates for reproduction. Later, as couples rear children together, their attention naturally shifts and expands to handle these increased responsibilities. And then, as two people age together, a romantic and sexual connection works to keep love alive and keep them young.

Little by little over this lifetime cycle, the brain circuits that fueled initial attraction give way to the chemicals and neural pathways of long-term love relationships and extended families. In the process, our most fundamental human bond—between two partners united for sexual gratification, childrearing, mutual affection, protection, and personal growth—is forever transformed.

The Least You Need to Know

- A woman's sexual desire often peaks at ovulation and immediately prior to her menstrual period.
- Men's dominance hierarchies are distinct, hormonally, from those of women.
- A man's desire for sex is highest in the morning and lowest at midday.

Enhancers and Detractors

In the next three chapters, we take on the myths and realities behind foods, herbs, street drugs, and lifestyle choices we associate with good or bad sex. We get to the bottom line about chocolate and ginseng, alcohol, and tobacco, to see which, if any, of these has any influence on your sexual desire or performance.

There is science to lend support to the libido-building effects of some age-old aphrodisiacs. And there's research to debunk long-held myths and folklore about certain animal parts, herbs, and street drugs long believed to aid male sexual performance.

What about stress and sex? It turns out to be a double-edged sword. The same goes for exercise. Like Goldilocks sitting at the dining table of the three bears, there's too much, too little, and just the right amount when it comes to how much you ingest or do to affect your love chemistry.

Sex Enhancers

In This Chapter

- Why certain foods and spices prime your sexual desire and performance
- What the ancients knew about love potions—and why they were outlawed
- The reward circuit of after-dinner sex

To discover the secrets behind sex enhancers, we need only keep in mind the basic chemistry of attraction. Anything that gives a push to the chemicals behind romantic infatuation, be it animal, mineral, or vegetable, can intensify your sexual urges. For example, chocolate, because of the PEA in the cocoa plant from which it is made, has long been regarded as an aphrodisiac. Never mind that you have to eat a box or two to feel much of a PEA punch.

If you're willing to try something ancient, unproven, and even dangerous, you may wish to ingest certain parts of the sperm whale or a beetle known as the Spanish fly. The lore surrounding these bizarre natural agents says they boost male libido—if they don't kill you first.

Sex enhancers may be found in food and drink, or they may drop out of thin air, in the form of a romantic memory or an association with a scent or a song. From any of these chemical or emotional sources, sex may naturally get a boost. At the very least, you can treat your senses while experimenting.

How They Work

Lest we forget … chemical reactions influence your emotions and emotions alter your chemistry. This is why placebos can work in controlled studies up to 30 or 40 percent of the time. And it's why the brain of an in-love man or woman lights up with activity from just seeing a lover's photo. This tells you that the most direct way to a man or woman's heart is to work the "romance receptors" in his or her love chemistry, wherein also lies the spark of sexual desire. And food and spices are just another way to get to these cells.

On Men

It's fairly simple: testosterone is the elixir of male desire, but improved circulation improves his erectile response. You can consider anything that increases circulation an enhancer and anything that constricts it an inhibitor, for both men and women; see Chapter 11 for those details.

The use of aphrodisiacs to enhance sex is an ancient practice, with new scientific discoveries only adding to their popularity. For example, recent research has created a buzz around a naturally occurring amino acid called l-arginine, which has been shown to increase circulation to the penis by enlarging the blood vessels. L-arginine is considered a precursor to nitric oxide, the reactive agent in erectile dysfunction medications. It can be obtained by prescription and through certain foods. Those eatables rich in l-arginine include granola, oatmeal, peanuts, cashews, walnuts, green vegetables, root vegetables, garlic, ginseng, soybeans, chickpeas, and seeds.

Although most aphrodisiacs in history have been geared toward enhancing a man's desire and improving his sexual performance, the irony is that relatively few men need much help in either department, at least not until they reach their fifties. Just as Viagra is used by younger men for recreational purposes, sex enhancers have traditionally been oriented more for a man's amusement than his physical need.

Of course, the question of what turns someone on is at least as subjective as it is objective. For the male of the species, who receives the most direct romantic cues from his eyes, an aphrodisiac is often something he can see. It can be sexy lingerie on a woman, the phallic shape of a banana, or the suggestion of a woman's vulva in a fig. To then bite into one of these fruits adds the fantasy of consuming that which you desire. Other fruits and vegetables, from asparagus to avocados, resemble male sex organs, at least in the eyes of those with sex on their minds. Other foods—eggs, for example—have traditionally been associated with fertility and retain a sexual connotation because of this link.

Sex enhancers reach their marks in a man by traveling one of two chemical pathways:

- Through his endocrine system, by increasing testosterone.

- Through his circulatory system, by increasing the amount of blood flowing to his genitals.

Men are also susceptible to scents. One stubborn belief surrounds the power of cooked cinnamon as a natural sexual stimulant for men. Psychiatrist Alan Hirsch, who had a special interest in discovering which scents can sexually arouse men and women, did extensive testing at his Smell and Taste Research Center in Chicago. He used penile and vaginal blood-flow measurements to determine which substances had the most impact on sexual desire. For men, he found that combinations of scents such as lavender and pumpkin pie had an unusually strong impact, increasing blood flow by up to 40 percent, while the combination of doughnuts and black licorice increased it by 31.5 percent. Other winners included cinnamon buns, buttered popcorn, and cheese pizza. One can imagine that Dr. Hirsch's laboratory often smelled like a men's college dormitory.

On Women

A woman is traditionally the one who likes to set the scene for love, be it with candles, a special meal, or perfumes. If sexual intercourse is the big draw for a man, romance is what attracts a woman—at least at first. Any sex enhancers geared toward women must feed their desire to be loved and adored.

How can you tell if a sex enhancer is working on a woman? A woman's heightened libido is prompted, like a man's, by the increased presence of testosterone (although in lower amounts) and by an increase in blood circulation to her genital organs. Female sexual desire is reflected and measurable by physical changes in the woman's body including these:

- Blood flow causing engorgement of her clitoris and labia

- Vaginal muscle contractions

- Dilated pupils

- Blushing of the cheeks and neck area

A woman's romance receptors are heavily congregated in her senses of touch and smell. She has a higher response to touch, due to the larger amount of oxytocin running through her body.

POINTER

Getting a woman in the mood for love is a no-brainer if you can enhance her craving for touch: give her a sensual massage; start with her feet, and then include her whole body.

When Dr. Hirsch tested females' vaginal blood-flow response to different smells, he discovered that men's colognes including the much-vaunted musk had zero or negative impact on women's arousal. On the positive side, he found lavender (again!), cucumber, licorice, and baby powder produced discernable positive arousal responses. Meanwhile, barbequed meat and cherries inhibit women's arousal.

As with men, recent studies have seen some improvement in blood flow to the genitals and thus increased arousal for women taking the amino acid l-arginine. Researchers at the University of Texas at Austin tested 24 post-menopausal women with l-arginine combined with Yohimbine, a natural stimulant extracted from bark from the Yohimbine tree, and found marked improvements in their blood flow up to an hour after taking this combination.

What Enhancers and Aphrodisiacs Can (and Can't) Do

There's a strong temptation to believe that if something has been considered an aphrodisiac for hundreds or thousands of years, there must be a good reason. Not true. Most larger mammals whose parts are mined for aphrodisiacal powers are the unfortunate casualties of this association between their size and ferocity and human sex enhancement. Science shows that it's wrong to believe that a man will become a better lover by imbibing a powdered rhinoceros horn.

But in some cases, long-held beliefs in the sexual-enhancing properties of certain plants and foodstuffs have been found to hold some truth. In the case of foods, such as chili peppers and fish rich in omega-3 fatty acids, the reasons for their staying power as aphrodisiacs likely have more to do with established positive influences on health, especially on sexual health. In modern times, these associations are considered less "magical" but no less positive.

The effects of aphrodisiacs are, by nature, transient. The most important thing that sex enhancers can't do is take the place of good sexual health.

Myths and Folklore

At least as far back as classical Greece, where the word aphrodisiac was coined in honor of the Goddess of Love, Aphrodite, societies took their aphrodisiacs and love potions very seriously. Although we've let the two run together in our modern minds, there's an important historical distinction to be made between them.

An aphrodisiac traditionally is a naturally derived substance a person imbibes in order to physically enhance his sexual desire or performance. Although an aphrodisiac may have been shared with one's lover or intended amour, it was intended to be recreational, evil, or underhanded. Among the most notorious aphrodisiacs in history are these:

- Ambrien, or ambergris, found in the digestive tract of the sperm whale, is still in use in some Arab countries. It is thought to work by increasing concentration of testosterone.

- Horny goat weed is a common hillside plant in Asia. According to legend, a shepherd noticed that goats grazing on this plant got friskier and sexually charged. Still in use today, its proponents say a chemical in horny goat weed functions much like Viagra and Cialis.

- The Spanish Fly was made of the ground-up, dried bodies of blister beetles; its power to excite and often kill the user had to do with rushing blood to the genitals and causing lethal irritation to the intestines. It's no longer a popular aphrodisiac, for obvious reasons.

Those who took such substances did so willingly. In contrast, a love potion was used in secret for manipulative ends; indeed, their use was also called witchcraft and made illegal in many places. In the 1500s, Venetians declared the use of love potions criminal. During the same century, a British royal, one Lady Grey, was publicly charged with bewitching King Edward IV by the use of "strange potions." Love potions often used ingredients intended to act as sedatives.

TURN-OFF

A modern equivalent of the Venetians' outlawed love potions are the illegal "date rape" drugs Rohypnol, GHB, and Ketamine. These synthesized substances are dropped surreptitiously in a woman's (and sometimes a man's) cocktail for the purpose of sexual assault. This happens without the woman having any memory of what took place.

Often the person who has unknowingly imbibed a date rape drug exhibits symptoms that suggests she is extremely drunk and the attacker offers to walk the victim somewhere safe. While there, the attacker sexually assaults the victim. What the ancient connivers and their modern counterparts apparently know was that these concoctions contain powerful ingredients capable of getting someone to do something she would normally consider outrageously out of character. Think of all the operas and Shakespearean plays that would be without peak drama if not for love potions used by the villain to seduce the desired man or woman for one night of illicit passion.

In the Pursuit of MORE

Unfortunately, despite the evidence to the contrary, many people around the world still believe that men gain sexual prowess from the horns, claws, and organs of animals. This most superstitious category of sex enhancers is also the one that puts some of the world's most endangered species, including the tiger, rhinoceros, elephant, and sperm whale, in unnecessary peril, given the spurious nature of these sexual enhancement claims.

And you only need open your spam filter to see that these claims and the marketing of such contraband substances continue to flourish, right alongside the ads for Viagra and penis enlargers.

Food and Love

From our mouths to the desire and pleasure centers of our brains, food and love share the same pathways and delights. Eating creates physiological changes in the body not unlike those that result from sexual arousal: an increase in pulse, circulation, temperature, and even sweat.

> **SEXY FACT**
>
> An immoderate use of chocolate was, in the seventeenth century, deemed so powerful an aphrodisiac that religious leaders strenuously enforced a ban forbidding monks and nuns from eating or drinking anything made with chocolate.

Chocolate

Chocolate contains phenylethylamine, PEA, the chemical compound that can produce feelings of euphoria by releasing dopamine, the brain chemical that also surges during orgasms.

Chocolate is a romantic mainstay. It's hard to imagine Valentine's Day without it. The so-called "love molecule" PEA is the chemical reason for it, although after centuries of association, we probably need only think of a box of chocolates to get the same effect. Apparently, the "zing" that comes from dark chocolate and cocoa is strongest, while the impact of white chocolate and coffee is less noticeable. Feel free to try this comparison test at home.

Other foods that, like chocolate, increase PEA and as a result are considered sex enhancers include: apples, tomatoes, almonds, cheddar cheese, and avocados.

Although not thought of in the same way as these other sexy foods, diet sodas—because of the PEA-simulating effects of their synthetic sugar substitutes, which can be converted to PEA in the bloodstream—can also be put in the same category as chocolates.

That said, consuming great quantities of diet soda or chocolate to get a PEA-inspired romantic rush is a very bad idea.

Fruits, Blooms, and Vegetables

The edible stems, roots, and flowers that have enjoyed many centuries of belief in their aphrodisiacal powers include these stalwart sprouts:

- Lilies
- Roses
- Violets
- Jasmine
- Melons
- Mandrake
- Yams
- Celery

Although some of these foods are thought to work their magic by being ingested, others, like roses and jasmine, affect us through their powerful, though subtle aromas.

The herb Asian ginseng has long been thought to have libido and sexual performance–building capabilities when ingested by men. Laboratory tests with rats given this herb showed increased sexual activity. It is thought that ginseng's effects may be due to its excitatory impact on the central nervous system. Ginseng doesn't have FDA approval for any of these uses.

Indigenous cultures of the Americas, the Far East, and Turkey have reportedly put much stock in the sexually stimulating properties of the hemp plant. According to travelers' accounts, the seeds and leaves of several species of hemp were chewed to increase a man's vigor and stamina for prolonged sexual intercourse.

In some cases hemp was combined with ambergris, musk, and sugar to sweeten and intensify the experience. These reports of extensive hemp use as sexual stimulants came primarily from eighteenth- and nineteenth-century European observers of the "Indians" who used them, and thus must be taken with a grain of salt. Some of these accounts claimed that when exotic birds of these regions were fed the same hemp seeds, their behavior also became "amorous."

Spices

As a stimulant for the circulatory system, ginger is said to increase blood flow to the genitals. Cinnamon is another widely revered aphrodisiac in the spice family. Asian societies also favor nutmeg as an aphrodisiac.

SEXY FACT

Certain spices are believed to improve the taste of semen and thus be advantageous for consumption by men who look forward to oral sex.

Some substances thought to spice up the taste of semen include …

- Cardamom
- Saffron
- Peppermint
- Lemon

Different foods and spices can change the taste of semen to what some consider a displeasing flavor. Some mentioned in this category include these:

- Garlic
- Onions
- Curry
- Asparagus

Chili peppers, used as a spice or eaten whole, are known for their burn. Capsaicin, the compound that gives chilies this effect, might also trigger the brain to release endorphins, which, at high levels, creates a sensation of pleasure. Apparently, chili peppers also stimulate the nervous system, which can, in turn, accentuate the effects of sexual arousal. This web of connectedness between body systems is an excellent reminder that sexual arousal is a whole-body experience.

Sex After Dinner—Why the Ritual

It's no secret that a romantic meal can put you in the mood for sex. So what makes a meal romantic? Three things: your intentions, the mood achieved by the setting, and the pure pleasures of eating.

A romantic dinner is, by definition, an intimate experience, a celebratory ritual just for the two of you. In a word, it's foreplay, especially if you've bathed and dressed with each other in mind. To maximize such an evening, all you need to do is find ways to enliven all five senses. Bring flowers, add some champagne, play music, and light some vanilla- or musk-scented candles, and you're much closer to getting your body and mind in the mood for love.

There's also a scientific perspective to lend to the natural pairing of food and sex. The human hunger for food and sex are basic drives, controlled by the reptilian area of the brain. Eating engages the same hypothalamus/amygdala/hippocamus circuit that is central to the chemistry of love. If you get one drive going, chances are good that the other will be waiting.

In addition, the reward center for food is connected to thousands of sense receptors on the tongue, and many more through your eyes and nasal passages. When these sense receptors are activated by seeing, eating, and smelling tasty foods, you are essentially warming up the same anticipation-and-reward system you'll be using after dinner when you and your partner have sex.

You should note that recipes using any of the aphrodisiacs covered in this chapter often call for a dollop or two of spirits or wine to wash them down. Red wine, known to aid heart health when consumed in moderation, no doubt helps loosen any lingering inhibitions about lovemaking.

The Chemistry of Erotica

The power of erotica depends on an observer and something sexy to observe. Of course, each person has a slightly different arousal chemistry and taste for visual stimuli. But in every case, erotica is something seen, not touched.

Even without touching the object of desire, for many people (including most men) erotica is a major enhancer of sexual desire. If we were to watch an fMRI brain scan of a male observer of erotic materials, his anticipation, memory, and pleasure circuit would be lighting up in much the same way it does when he anticipates real sex with a living, breathing partner.

As evolution shaped the human species, our sense of sight overtook the more primitive senses of smell and touch as central to sexual arousal. Sight is a much more complex process than smell. Sight involves the brain's frontal cortex and limbic system, and this more elaborate circuitry adds memory and conscious thought to the more basic processing of olfactory and skin stimuli. Visually, we can receive input from a greater distance than we can through either smell or touch.

Once a sexy visual stimulus is received, the same PEA and norepinephrine (the neurotransmitter that tells us to wake up and pay attention!) associated with "love at first sight" are set loose in the brain. Thus, our biochemistry makes erotic visual stimuli a highly potent aphrodisiac, as it has been for centuries.

Men, Erotica, and Arousal

Given the fact that men get turned on first by things they see, one thing men see a lot of today is pornography, especially online porn. Before the personal computer and home video, a man had to leave the house to get his erotica. Then and now, erotic art, nude dancers and strippers, and X-rated movies in theaters or private booths satisfied men's desire for sexual arousal at a distance.

Another difference between men's and women's taste in erotica is the level of sexual details preferred by men. Pornography aimed at men (in other words, most pornography) shows the sex act in vivid detail, with little or nothing left to the imagination. Plot, not so much.

Women, Erotica, and Arousal

Women generally like their erotica to emphasize sensuality and romance more than explicit sex. *Playgirl* magazine, though not explicit, never caught on like its big brother, *Playboy*. Many women simply get turned off by hardcore pornography.

When we say a woman's fantasies are contextual, we mean she sees erotica in an emotional and relationship context. Romance novels are the biggest category of books published in the world because of this preference by women readers. Although obstacles keep the star-crossed lovers apart for many pages in these books, at the story's climax they are without exception reunited to live "happily ever after." Research by Maryanne Fisher, author of this book, with Anthony Cox, has examined the words that appear in the titles of books by the largest romance fiction company, Harlequin. They examined every book published by the company, starting in 1949 and ending in June 2009, which yielded 22,794 titles. The top 20 words reveal themes of love, babies, and marriage, suggesting that women relate romance to issues of reproduction and commitment.

However you manage to get your infusions of PEA and the other love juices going, enjoy!

The Least You Need to Know

- Foods and spices that aid circulation are natural sex enhancers.
- Why do dinner and sex go together so well? Control of the involuntary drives for food and sex resides in the same hypo-thalamus/amygdalae/hippocamus circuit of the brain.
- Erotica holds appeal for men and women; men prefer details, whereas women get swayed by the emotional content.

Sex Inhibitors

In This Chapter

- Which street drugs can damage your sex life
- The foods that can dampen your libido
- Why too much dieting kills sexual desire

What you don't know about booze, cigarettes, street drugs, and other indulgences can have an adverse effect on your sexuality. Before that happens, why not use what you've learned thus far about the chemistry of love to separate the good stuff from the bad? Many illegal substances long thought to be aphrodisiacs, cocaine and opium for example, turn out to have an opposite, deleterious effect on sexual desire and performance.

You need a healthy body and brain to deliver the pleasures of sex. There must be enough blood circulation to bring oxygen and nutrients to all of the organs involved with sexual desire, arousal, and performance. Your sexuality involves your whole body, from your skin, lungs, and stomach, to the processing centers of your brain. The heavy use of alcohol, nicotine, and cocaine has been shown to cause erection problems in men.

Skip this chapter at your own peril.

Chemical Depressants

The body is a finely tuned machine that doesn't appreciate being messed with. And yet, that's what people routinely do, sometimes operating under the mistaken belief that they're ingesting something that will expand their sexual pleasures. There are many culprits. Depressants as a category produce fleeting sensations of euphoria, but they achieve this effect by dulling the senses, thereby diminishing your brain and body's reactions to pain and pleasure.

Alcohol—the False Enhancer

A drink or two relaxes you and then removes inhibitions for flirting, conversation, and, perhaps, sex. In fact, it has been shown that a small amount of alcohol ups oxytocin in your body. However, too much alcohol can take away from your performance and your ability to feel much at all, including an orgasm.

Anxiety Relief = Bad Choices

Obviously, intense social inhibitions and anxiety are sex inhibitors. However, while providing temporary relief from social anxiety, alcohol can depress hormones that regulate the chemistry of sex. One is DHEA, which, when operating normally, increases women's sex drive. Another is vasopressin, which plays a key role in a man's ability to achieve an erection. Vasopressin also supports clear thinking and the ability to avoid emotional or sexual extremes.

Too much and too frequent consumption of alcohol lowers oxytocin. This is the hormone that sensitizes and magnetizes a woman's sense of touch, so lowering it can contribute to lower libido and depressed arousal response in females.

Alcohol and Testosterone Depression

Studies have shown testosterone levels in men with alcoholism to be lower. Research has also shown that heavy alcohol use causes erection problems. These negative effects on their sexuality often persuade men to seek help for their alcoholism.

Other Negative and Long-Term Effects

Alcohol can become an addiction for anyone who abuses it over a sustained period of time, especially individuals who are genetically vulnerable due to their family history. An addiction to alcohol—like to other addictive substances including nicotine, cocaine, meth, and behaviors such as gambling—literally hijacks the brain's reward system. This locks the addict into a debilitating cycle of anticipation and reward that is difficult to break.

According to neuroscientist and psychiatrist Daniel Amen, M.D., author of *The Brain in Love*, long-term alcohol dependence, which he defines as the daily drinking of more than two servings of wine (6 oz.), beer (12 oz.), or liquor (1.5 oz.), is bad for healthy relationships. It damages and dulls parts of the brain involved with forethought and impulse control as well as memory.

Many people with common mental health disorders such as depression, ADD, or one of the anxiety disorders, use alcohol to self-medicate the symptoms of these disorders. But any relief they receive is temporary. The trade-off is a worsening of symptoms. Alcohol is known to increase symptoms of depression. If someone is drinking and taking prescribed medication for depression or anxiety, alcohol can lessen the serotonin-, dopamine-, or norepinephrine-boosting effects of the medication, also negatively impacting sexuality.

Nicotine

Nicotine is found in cigarettes, cigars, chewing tobacco, and nicotine patches. The reports on nicotine and the quality of your sex life bring a lot more bad news.

Even if you wait until after your orgasm to light up a cigarette, that smoke can still mess with your performance the next time around. Tobacco causes blood vessels to constrict and decreases flow to vital organs, among them the brain and the penis. This is why an addiction to cigarettes is associated with impotence in men. A curious exception to this finding came in one early study of women, which correlated the number of cigarettes smoked with the women's reported intensity of orgasm. This was thought to indicate a possible association between nicotine's dopamine-stimulating effects.

Generally speaking, tobacco is considered a net negative in terms of sex appeal and performance. The circulatory constriction caused by nicotine blocks blood flow to the skin cells, making skin age faster. So if we put it all together, nicotine can be blamed for a reduction in sex appeal, bad breath, and poor sexual performance.

Marijuana

About 40 percent of Americans have used marijuana at least once, and it remains the most prevalently used illicit drug. Some estimates put regular users at 10 percent of the population. The source of marijuana is the hemp plant (*Cannabis Sativa*). The psychoactive ingredients are THC, which is primarily responsible for the high, and other cannabinoids found in the leaves and flowering shoots of the plant. Hashish is a potent form of cannabis usually taken from the resin that is found on the flowering tops of female plants. It contains the highest amount of THC.

You may feel the effects of marijuana within seconds to several minutes after breathing in the smoke (from a rolled cigarette or a pipe), or within 30 to 60 minutes after eating foods containing marijuana, such as "hash brownies."

The main effects of marijuana are on behavior, because the drug affects the central nervous system (CNS). Marijuana gives people a feeling of joy (euphoria); relaxation; and enhanced sight, hearing, and taste with low to moderate doses. Most users also report an increase in their appetite ("the munchies"). Small amounts of marijuana are known to enhance sexual arousal by increasing PEA. However, it may be a case of "less is more," as a regular intake of marijuana or hashish has been shown to cause a loss of short-term memory and lower libido.

Other unpleasant effects of marijuana that may occur in regular users include lack of orientation, changed body image, and severe paranoia. Marijuana has specific effects that may decrease your ability to perform tasks that require a lot of coordination (such as driving a car). It affects visual tracking and prolongs the sense of time. Marijuana also decreases motivation for goal-directed activities. The drug can affect learning because it can reduce your ability to concentrate and pay attention. Studies have shown that learning may become "state-dependent," meaning that information learned while under the influence of marijuana is best remembered in the same state of drug influence. Regular users, when they stop marijuana use, may have withdrawal effects.

Studies done around the world have conclusively shown that heavy marijuana use by young people, especially those under the age of 16, can trigger psychosis in genetically vulnerable individuals. This refers to those with a family history of mental illness, especially the major psychiatric diseases of bipolar disorder and schizophrenia.

Heroin and Barbiturates

Much of what is known about the effects of narcotic drugs, including heroin, which is derived from opium, comes from the study of naturally occurring opioids such as the brain's calm-producing endorphins. Scientists found that some of the body's opiate receptors are located on the frontal lobes of the cerebral cortex, highlighting a possible reason for the diminished powers of information processing caused by the use of opiates. There are also opiate receptors in deeper parts of the brain that process pain and emotion.

This research has also established conclusively that abuse of opioids leads to sexual problems. In men, long-term opioid or other narcotic use leads to loss of libido, and erectile dysfunction. If he experiences an erection, a man may be unable to achieve orgasm.

It is believed that sustained use of opioids produces a decrease in hormones, including testosterone. This reduction can do the most harm to a man's sexual functioning. Women who become addicted to narcotics such as heroin also experience decreased libido, and anorgasmia.

Painkillers or barbiturates as a class of drugs, whether legally prescribed or illegally obtained, will restrict blood flow to the brain. This deprives the brain of nutrients, gradually numbing the processing of emotional and physical sensations that are central to the chemistry of sex and love.

Chemical Stimulants

Synthetic chemicals that stimulate the brain, nervous system, and circulatory system can provide a short-term euphoria that fuels sex drive and performance. But there's a high price to pay for this short-term high. Regular users of amphetamine or methamphetamine (also called speed) become single-mindedly interested in obtaining their next high, which becomes increasingly difficult to sustain. Their mind and other senses are dulled. Another word for this state is "burnout."

Although their use has been shown to increase stamina and facilitate orgasm, the chronic use of cocaine or amphetamines induces sexual disorders and anorgasmia in a high proportion of addicts. Among the worst effects of synthetic chemical stimulants is their potential to trigger symptoms similar to paranoid schizophrenia.

Cocaine/Crack

Cocaine increases PEA and dopamine activity and it's commonly believed to enhance sexual pleasure. Low doses may in fact do so by activating the brain's reward system and delaying ejaculation. However, regular use of cocaine is detrimental to men's and women's sexual performance and libido.

In one study, 30 percent of male users reported that it impaired ejaculation, and 80 percent of females reported that it reduced sexual enjoyment. It is thought that the negative impact of cocaine on penile erections results from its *vasoconstrictive* effects. Long-term use of cocaine can create anorgasmia and low sexual desire.

DEFINITION

Vasoconstriction is the narrowing (constriction) of blood vessels by muscles in their walls. When blood vessels constrict, the flow of blood is restricted or slowed.

Speed

Methamphetamine, or meth, is a highly addictive drug, whether injected, snorted, or smoked. It affects the brain and central nervous system by blocking the reuptake of the naturally stimulating neurotransmitter norepinephrine, leaving more of it in the synapses of the brain.

In a similar way it also increases the level of dopamine. When methamphetamine is injected or smoked, it immediately produces an intensely pleasurable sensation by releasing high levels of dopamine in the brain. Snorting methamphetamine produces a similar but less intense euphoric sensation.

Methamphetamine is a highly addictive drug, capable of doing severe harm to its regular users. Even taken in small amounts, methamphetamine can dangerously increase heart rate and blood pressure. It commonly lowers appetite and causes sleeplessness. In a heavy user, meth is capable of bringing about cardiovascular collapse. Other effects of longer-term use on the central nervous system include chronic anxiety, tremors, paranoia, aggressiveness, and insomnia.

Ecstasy

Ecstasy (also called MDMA) is similar to methamphetamines but it produces different subjective and physiological effects. Primarily, it produces a powerful effect on the user's social and sexual responses, increasing sociability, sexual feelings, and positive mood. Its stimulating, euphoric, and hallucinogenic properties have made MDMA increasingly popular with adolescents over the past two decades. This chemical affects the user's brain by causing the concentrated release of the neurotransmitters dopamine, norepinephrine, and serotonin.

The flooding of serotonin caused by MDMA likely causes the mood-elevating effects experienced by users. Other effects include increased tactile sensitivity; empathic feelings; hyperthermia; increased heart rate, blood pressure, metabolism; as well as feelings of exhilaration, energy, and increased mental alertness. These affects can bring about a temporary sense of enhanced sensual and sexual experience in the user.

During the 1970s and 1980s, prior to the criminalization of MDMA, some psychotherapists and psychologists experimented with the use of this drug with patients dealing with emotional trauma (PTSD, post-traumatic stress disorder) with some reported success.

Research done in 2001 on the effects of this drug on users showed that it moderately to significantly increased libido in 90 percent of men and women tested. However, penile erection was impaired in 40 percent of the men. Orgasms, which were frequently delayed under the influence of ecstasy, were subjectively considered to be more intense.

The dangers of ecstasy are primarily associated with its frequent recreational use especially by young adults, whose brains are at sensitive developmental stages. By releasing large amounts of serotonin, MDMA causes the brain to become significantly depleted of this neurotransmitter, contributing to the negative after-effects that users often experience for several days after taking the drug. Some documented negative effects include impaired memory and learning, rapid or irregular heartbeat, reduced appetite, dehydration, heart failure, and the onset of or increased symptoms of depression.

Speed and ecstasy production and distribution are now illegal in the United States.

Foods That Can Inhibit Sexual Function

Food and lifestyle choices have long been understood as having a direct impact on sexuality, at times a dulling one. Plato and Aristotle advocated a "cool regimen" in every respect, including the custom of going barefoot, taking cold baths, and eating cold foods, as means of checking overabundant carnal desire.

The foodstuffs believed in days of old to have this "refrigerating" effect on sex drive included infusions from the leaves or flowers of the white water-lily (*Nymphea Alba*), lettuce, violets, endive (*Cichorium Endivia*), cucumbers, the juice of lemons, and vinegar and drops of hemlock and camphor. (The latter are not recommended for home use!)

Another fascinating belief still in vogue in eighteenth- and nineteenth-century Europe advocated the study of mathematics as a means to dampen "assaults of vice and libidinousness." The theorem went that all those big, abstract ideas filling one's mind when learning trigonometry and calculus left no room for sexual desire.

Advice based on this belief appeared in contemporary manuals of proper behavior. As recorded in his *Confessions*, one older woman said to the young and sexually prolific Jean-Jacques Rousseau, "James, give up the ladies, and apply yourself to mathematics."

With the help of newer science, we can add a biochemical perspective to age-old beliefs about which foods and lifestyle choices put a damper on healthy, pleasurable sex. We can also understand the sexual implications of the impact on our bodies of eating too much or too little.

High Fats

Too much saturated fat can, over time, clog arteries and prevent an adequate flow of blood from reaching the genital region. This not only interferes with the ability to perform sexually, but also inhibits sexual pleasure.

We also know that an excess of fatty foods (such as too much dairy and meat), especially in combination with regular alcohol consumption, can create an overtaxed liver. If a woman's liver cannot properly accomplish its monthly flushing of estrogen from her system, this can then aggravate the physical and emotional symptoms of PMS by causing an imbalance in the woman's hormones. Insomuch as a serious case of PMS dampens a woman's sex drive, this type of diet acts as an inhibitor. By reducing alcohol intake and adding more B_6 and magnesium available in whole grains and green vegetables, PMS systems may be lessened, and sex improved.

Too little fat in your diet is also to be avoided because fat plays a role in producing hormones after it's metabolized in the liver. Olive oil, salmon, and nuts are optimal sources of these "good" fats.

Fasting, Famine, and Restrictive Diets

Lack of proper nutrition negatively impacts a woman's estrogen level. Estrogen helps maintain a woman's sex drive, promotes vaginal lubrication, maintains skin tone, and prevents depression. When dieting to excess and/or taking diet pills wreak havoc with a woman's estrogen level, it can cause lower libido. Dieting also lowers serotonin, and, along with her lower estrogen, can contribute to depression.

A girl or woman who is malnourished—whether due to poverty or an eating disorder such as anorexia nervosa—will see her menstrual periods stop, indicating a breakdown of the female hormonal cycle. Research suggests that women need a minimum amount of body fat to ovulate, which is why professional marathon runners, who have little body fat, tend to be infertile. There will also be a suppression of her sexual desire and response.

At the other extreme, being overweight is also a sex inhibitor. Obesity increases blood pressure, which is another cause of decreased libido in men and women.

According to Dr. Ridwan Shabsigh, director of the New York Center for Human Sexuality and associate professor of urology at Columbia University's medical school, "There has been very solid research showing that obesity is a risk factor for erectile dysfunction and low testosterone. Reducing weight results in an increase of testosterone, and thus an increase in sexual function."

The Least You Need to Know

- Depressants such as alcohol and barbiturates slow the brain and the body, eventually destroying libido and putting other body systems at high risk.
- Stimulant drugs like cocaine and methamphetamine constrict blood vessels, thus dampening sex and putting the user at risk for stroke and heart problems.
- Eating too much or too little can squash your sex drive and performance.

Staying Fit for Sex

Chapter 15

In This Chapter

- What figs, oysters, avocados, and chili peppers might do to enhance your sexual health
- Why the couple who works out together has better sex
- The connection between low female libido and exercise

If you haven't already, it's time to expand your knowledge of sexuality beyond the genital universe, especially when it comes to staying fit for sex. Your entire body and mind need to be in reasonably good shape to have a satisfying sexual experience. On these pages, we cover some of the flash points of your sexual health. Getting them right will help put you just where you want to be: in someone's loving arms.

Nutrition

The best way to enhance your sex life is to get your blood going. You'll need nutrients from eating all the basic food groups in three balanced meals a day. If you're not getting the necessary vitamins and minerals from meals and healthy snacks, you'll want to supplement with multi-vitamins. Here are some basic nutritional guidelines with your sexual health in mind.

You Are What You Eat

Circulation-enhancing dishes are the foods that help blood reach all the body's organs from your heart to your liver to the genitals and the brain. Some of the best eatables for circulation include those high in omega-3 fatty acids such as flax, walnuts, mackerel, and wild salmon. Fish oils are also available as a nutritional supplement.

Carbohydrates play a vital role in keeping you energized and your organs functioning properly. Some carbs are not fattening or harmful. The bad rap given to eating carbs does not apply to whole grains such as whole-wheat bread, pasta, or brown rice.

 TURN-OFF

"White carbs" like white bread, white rice, and white sugar are considered empty calories. These refined carbohydrates give you a jump-start, but then your energy can quickly peter out. Plus, white carbs are more likely to pack on the pounds.

Vegetables and fruits will help lower cholesterol levels, and help keep blood moving. Eating more fruits and vegetables contributes to weight loss because, relative to other food groups, they are low in calories and high in fiber, which makes you feel full.

Because obesity is associated with low testosterone levels, anything you do to ensure proper body mass will help maintain your sex drive.

Vitamins and Minerals for Optimal Nutrition

Certain foods are important because they supply vitamins, minerals, and enzymes important to sexual health. Others support the production or utilization of hormones in the body. Here is a sample of foods and herbs that are considered sexual health boosters, and how they provide support.

- Figs, rich in amino acid
- Pineapples, containing the enzyme bromelain, thought to increase male libido

- Oysters, rich in zinc, a mineral used in the production of testosterone

- Avocados, rich in B_6, which also increases male hormone production

- Chili peppers, which have a stimulating effect on nerve endings and heart rate, and so assist circulation

- Prunes, dates, and raisins contain the mineral boron, which helps the body utilize estrogen

- Garlic, another food that improves blood flow

- Ginkgo bilboa, from the Chinese ginkgo tree, an antioxidant that supports circulation, although not FDA-approved for medicinal use

- Soy, in soybeans, sprouts, and tofu, is known to be a selective estrogen receptor modulator (SERM). This means that soy can selectively stimulate or inhibit responses similar to estrogen on body tissue. For example, soy helps the vagina stay lubricated and combats symptoms of menopause, like hot flashes. Studies have shown that soy is also beneficial to the prostate, a crucial part to men's reproductive system.

The bottom line in order to have a body fit for sex is maintaining moderation in all you eat and drink. Watch quantities. Most people gain weight because they make no distinction in the amount of food on their plate. Size matters, whether it's a burger or bowl of ice cream. No one feels like having sex when they've stuffed themselves to the gills; a nap is more likely to follow dinner.

Sleep

Sleep deprivation decreases blood circulation and brain activity, and it can be a factor in low sex drive. Not everyone needs the same number of hours of sleep, although research has shown a minimum of seven hours per night to be optimum for the average adult. To be healthy enough for sex, each of us must have at least the minimum amount of deep, restful sleep.

It seems our overscheduled, stress-filled modern lives are taking a big toll on our chances of getting a night of sound sleep, or enough satisfying sex. According to Dr. Laura Berman, director of the Berman Center for Women's Sexual Health, "What ends up happening is that you try to pack too much in. You get into bed. You're stressed. You're uptight. And then you start getting stressed about not being able to fall asleep, and that keeps you even more sleepless. Instead, you should try having sex. It will help you sleep, because it releases endorphins and you feel better about yourself."

Food and drinks or drugs that cause sleeplessness, including anything containing caffeine (coffee, tea, cola sodas), are going to cost you sleep and detract from sex. They'll do this by depleting your energy and decreasing circulation. People with dark bags under their eyes for lack of sleep are not going to look their best, either.

Overeating will also deplete your energy, and make you sleepy and/or too full for sex.

Illness and Chronic Diseases

Men and women who suffer from diseases like diabetes, high blood pressure, arthritis, and cancer are at a higher risk of low libido than those without. Treatments such as chemotherapy and commonly prescribed medications can also take a heavy toll on libido and performance. Beyond any direct impact these diseases or their treatment may have on the biochemistry of sex, many chronic diseases cause stress and leave the body feeling fatigued.

Allergies

New medical research regularly sheds light on sexual complications brought on by diseases and conditions that had not previously been studied with sexual effects in mind. One such recurring condition with many sufferers, as many as 10 to 40 percent of the American population, is the common allergy known as hay fever, with the medical name allergic rhinitis.

When polled, 83 percent of over 700 people with this allergy said it affected their sexual activity at least sometimes, with almost 18 percent of those affected saying their allergies nearly always got in the way of a satisfying sex life. Exactly why the allergies affect sexual functioning isn't certain, but researchers suspect that the runny nose, itchy eyes, and other symptoms can make a person feel distracted and less than sexy. The good news is that over-the-counter and prescription treatments for allergies and hay fever can lessen or eliminate many of their symptoms, so sufferers need not feel without recourse, and they should certainly not feel alone.

Mental Health Disorders

Mild or clinical depression and any one of the common anxiety disorders (including OCD, panic disorder, ADHD, and anorexia) can also squash sex drive. They do this by interfering with the sex and mood hormones (including serotonin, dopamine, norepinephrine, oxytocin, and serotonin), thereby destabilizing the chemistry of sex and love.

It also doesn't help that the most popular class of medications used to treat depression and anxiety, the SSRIs (including Prozac, Paxil, and Zoloft), have been known to decrease libido. Fortunately, alternative antidepressant and antianxiety medications haven't been shown to negatively impact sex drive. Be sure to speak to your doctor about any side effects you experience, and also share any life changes, like the beginning or end of a relationship, moving, a new job, family issues, and other things that may be affecting your mental and/or physical health.

SEXY FACT

Continual exercise on horseback was considered by Hippocrates to be anti-aphrodisiacal for men. His concerns were reportedly the continual joltings and compression produced upon the male genital organs, which, he feared, could prevent an erection altogether. Sorry, we couldn't find any surveys of the sex lives of real cowboys to see how it's worked out for them.

Exercise

As you consider the benefits of nutrition and exercise for your sex life, keep this fact in mind: a healthy body and satisfying sex are wholly interdependent on each other. You can't have one without the other, at least not for long.

The reason is that the body's organs and systems are interconnected. For example, the *receptors* for estrogen and testosterone, the "Mama" and "Papa" of sex hormones, are not restricted to the genital organs or even the brain. They're all over your body.

DEFINITION

Receptors are the exterior cellular structures that can bind with the molecules of the hormones and neurotransmitters in the chemistry of love and draw them into the cell. Receptors and hormones are like locks and keys; any receptor only binds with a single chemical. The others will pass right by.

When exercise activates the sensory fibers in the muscles and joints— for example, when you swing your tennis racket—oxytocin and endorphins are released in the brain. Do it frequently enough, and oxytocin cues the release of dopamine, which triggers testosterone. These hormones then go about the business of activating your sex drive—from head to toe.

Your emotions, so integral to the chemistry of love, begin as organic changes in the body's sensory neurons, those stirrings in your feet, stomach, skin, and eyes. The chemical reactions these neurons create in your central nervous and endocrine systems manifest physically in your pounding heart, tight stomach, sweaty palms, and tensed muscles. In effect, they're telling your brain what to think about what's happening in your inner and outer worlds.

So should all you couch potatoes get up and start moving? Yes, of course, so you will look good, feel good, and think better. But don't forget, perhaps, the equally important reason: to have better sex. Working out and working up a sweat increases your libido, thus making sex more frequent. The icing on the cake: the sex you and your partner have with your fit bodies will be much more satisfying.

How a Workout Primes Arousal

Physical exertion over a sustained period of time causes the release of endorphins in the brain. This is what athletes call the "runner's high," as endorphins are the brain's natural opiates. There is some research to indicate that this increase in endorphins stimulates sex hormones.

Exercise activates the elevated mood and state of calm physically indicated by lower heart rate, more effective digestion, lower stress hormone, and lower blood pressure. This combined increase of endorphins and oxytocin is why we feel good after going to the gym. The more you exercise, the more long-lasting these effects are.

For men and especially for women, the increased presence of oxytocin and endorphins in your body and brain will increase your sense of well-being, which makes you want to cuddle and connect with your partner. For a woman who experiences low libido, exercise does even more.

Exercise for Low Female Libido

As many as 40 percent of women complain about having a low sex drive at some point in their lives, and a survey out of the University of Chicago found that about 33 percent of women ages 18 to 59 complain of a low libido. The problem is there are dozens of reasons why a woman of any age may experience a low sex drive—although "low" can be difficult to define. According to researchers, people in their twenties have sex an average of 112 times a year—a number that drops to 86 times per year for people in their thirties and 69 times a year for people in their forties. This decline in sexual activity over time is considered normal.

Research has shown that women who exercise regularly tend to have more active and satisfying sex lives. They're more quickly aroused and reach orgasm faster than those who don't work out. Your exercise regimen doesn't have to include running a marathon. It is thought that less vigorous and nonaerobic exercise including yoga also assists sexual health by stimulating blood flow to the genitals.

In one recent study, sex researchers showed an erotic film to college-age women after a session of strenuous exercise to test its affect on their sexual arousal. They showed the same film to women who did not exercise prior to watching it. The group who exercised showed higher levels of arousal than the one who didn't. Arousal was measured by a physical test for vaginal muscle contractions and with self-questionnaires.

Stress as Libido Dampener

Women, especially, are susceptible to the presence of anxiety in their lives putting the damper on sexual desire and/or the ability to reach orgasm. For most women, it's easier to get turned on once the brain, especially her fear and worry center in the amygdala, is turned off. Any lingering concerns about work, the kids, or bills can torpedo her drive, arousal, and orgasm, even in the middle of intercourse.

In *The Female Brain*, neuropsychiatrist Louann Brizendine suggests this "extra neurological step" for women in having to free themselves of mundane concerns before settling into sex may be the reason why it often takes women 3 to 10 times longer than men to reach orgasm.

What you may have observed in the course of everyday relationships has now been studied in the laboratory. In various studies, researchers have found that women's arousal is facilitated under certain conditions and not others. A woman gets turned on most easily when she is …

- Deeply "in love" and/or in the attraction phase of a relationship
- In a trusting, committed relationship
- Physically comfortable and warm
- Given 10 minutes of foreplay
- Not angry at her partner
- Satisfied with the appearance of her body

When given brain scans under controlled conditions where conflict was represented visually to both male and female subjects, women's brains registered the stress of conflict more deeply and pervasively than did the men's brains. Evolutionary psychologists believe this difference evolved from early woman's need to perceive more subtle threats to herself and her children, while her mate worried about bigger ones. Unlike a woman, conflict can get a man's sexual "juices" going, meaning his testosterone. He will not feel the need to respond or get "stressed out" over a conflict unless he's physically threatened by someone.

POINTER

Sex researchers sometimes say that foreplay for a woman is everything that happens in the 24 hours preceding sex. For a man, it's everything in the three minutes before. So gentlemen and ladies, it's best to get any fights resolved well before playtime.

Anxiety and Sexual Arousal

Andrea Bradford and Cindy Meston at the University of Texas, Austin, carried out novel research on the impact of women's anxiety on their sexual arousal. Once again, in this study a sexually explicit film was shown to subjects in a laboratory to induce sexual arousal. Physical arousal was measured by using VPA or vaginal pulse amplitude; subjective arousal was ascertained with a questionnaire.

In the study involving 38 female participants, the researchers measured each woman's physical and subjective sexual response while each was under the influence of *state anxiety* to see how they would respond to the erotic film stimulus. Bradford and Meston found the highest physical sexual response from the women with a moderate amount of state anxiety. However, this greater physical arousal score did not repeat with women who had either very high or very low state anxiety going into the test.

DEFINITION

State anxiety is an acute but transitory emotional response of apprehension comparable to the kind of anxiety someone acquires in the course of a stressful day.

In fact, for both categories, the women's physical arousal responses were very low. Meanwhile, women with low, moderate, and high trait anxiety had no discernable positive or negative subjective responses to the erotic film. These results appear to suggest that approaching sex with some anxiety is a potential turn-on, while too much is definitely not. Having no anxiety at all makes no difference for the woman when faced with a sexual stimulus.

Men generally have an easier time getting aroused and climaxing, even when they're feeling a lot of stress. As long as blood flows to the penis and leads to an erection, he's generally good to go, unimpeded all the way to orgasm.

Sex as Stress-Buster

Forget sleeping pills or tranquilizers. The answer to stress is a kiss; if that kiss leads to more, so much the better. Sex researcher and popular author Laura Berman recently reported the results of a large-scale study on intimacy in which she found sexual satisfaction worked for a majority of men and women as a stress reliever. The same study found that couples who kiss regularly and spontaneously have not only a higher level of intimacy, but also enjoyed decreased levels of stress and depression in their lives.

Finally, it's worth noting the growing conclusive research demonstrating the health benefits of regular sex. It improves mood, memory, and overall health. One study made the claim that regular sex reduced the risk for a heart attack or stroke by 50 percent. And it's known that regular sex also increases the level of testosterone in both men and women. Thus, regular sex leads to more sex. If you follow some of the other sexual health and fitness advice in this chapter, more sex will also mean better sex.

Meditate for Better Sex

There's a good reason for the integration in eastern spiritual traditions, especially Indian Hindu and Chinese Taoism, of meditative and sexual practices. Tantra, as in tantric sex, is a form of Hindu religion that taught specific sexual positions for the attainment of maximum spiritual development and sexual experience. Simply put, in these traditions, sex enhances spirituality, and vice versa. As an indication of their effectiveness, many of these tantric sexual practices have enjoyed a renaissance and remain popular in mainstream Western cultures today.

With or without the sexual component, meditation is a form of yoga that teaches practitioners to quiet the mind and body in order to center oneself by attuning and calming the self. Some practices include focus on breathing, mantras, and posture control. In Western spiritual traditions, a similar effect can be reached through prayer. The key is turning off your conscious awareness of the things large and small that capture your attention in the course of the day.

Neuropsychiatrist Daniel Amen participated in a brain-scan study of the impact of an 18-minute chanting meditation, and reported in his book *The Brain in Love* that it showed an increase in activity in the prefrontal lobes, as opposed to the parietal lobes. He interpreted this result as "tuning within," not out. As a result of this form of meditation, Amen also saw increased activity in the right temporal lobe, an area of the brain associated with processing thoughts and emotions related to spirituality and sexuality.

Interestingly, this same right side of the brain helps people process music, rhythm, rituals, beauty, and pictures, rather than the words, judgments, and linear thoughts of the left side. It follows, then, that anything that stimulates this part may also facilitate the chemistry of love and romance.

The Least You Need to Know

- Good circulation, achieved through proper nutrition, exercise, and good sleep habits, is the key to sexual good health.
- Regular sex, even regular kissing, can reduce stress.
- Women, much more than men, get sidetracked from sex by everyday worries.

Friends, Foes, and Family

Everything you've learned about the chemistry of love between romantic partners will now reappear in your other relationships, from best friends to worst foes. It's there when you go gaga over the new baby. It's all over your workplace and everywhere you play or socialize, on the basketball court and softball field. Don't forget church or a boy's night out. Love it or hate it, chemistry is life.

Other Relationships

Chapter 16

In This Chapter

- How primal instincts and chemistry work together to shape the modern workplace and ball field
- What a women's dormitory has in common with a harem
- The science behind a woman's intuition

This is where we look at your chemistry with anyone who isn't a family member or a romantic partner. But don't be surprised that the same chemical players that prompt a mother to suckle her baby or spark romantic longings for a sweetheart reappear in these relationships, albeit for different purposes. You may be thrown for a loop as we reveal the chemical reactions that rule your everyday life at work, school, and in social groups, with friends and foes alike.

Chemistry with Friends

To explore why certain people become your close friends and others don't, and why some people have the power to repel you, we need to call on body chemistry, gender differences, and evolutionary psychology. Our human habits of living in family groups, which eventually expanded beyond blood relations to clans and tribes and then nations, were formed starting a million years ago or more.

The body chemistry that evolved to support the primal needs of early humans was then and remains today entirely practical. Those men, women, and children bonded together for greater safety, to obtain and share food, to trade with and learn from each other, and to perform the rituals that have reflected the aspirations of every human culture. But wait, you say; eking out survival on the African savannah bears no resemblance to my modern, take-out-dinner lifestyle.

Don't be so quick to dismiss the social habits of prehistoric humans as irrelevant to your own. The patterns that survive in our social relationships today have been shaped by eons and were advantageous to those who displayed them. So with that in mind, let's take a closer look at what's driving our social lives, beginning with those people we call our friends.

Touch and Friends

Much of what feels good about friendship begins with oxytocin, the hormone that magnetizes contact both physical and emotional. Oxytocin creates a sense of calm in a person and connection between people. And while women have more of it because its production is triggered by estrogen, men receive the bonding benefits of oxytocin, too. It's just that with men, the more individualistic, competitive inclinations of testosterone are also at play, even when a man is at rest.

The physical sensation of touch on the skin triggers the production of oxytocin in the hypothalamus. This chemical then travels through the central nervous system and into the bloodstream to receptors located throughout the body. The stimulus for oxytocin release can take the form of a hug, a kiss on the cheek, or a hand on a knee.

POINTER

A person who is touched is more likely to honor a promise. This could be how the social practice of two people shaking hands on an agreement evolved. So the next time you make a deal, be sure to shake on it.

The internal chemical experience of touch can also be triggered by nonphysical intimate connection, like the kind of contact you experience when you share a confidential conversation with a friend. Once it gets going in the brain, oxytocin tends to keep on pumping. There isn't an automatic shut-off valve. When this hormone is triggered often, as in very touchy-feely friendships like those between many female friends, the feelings of calm and connection remain longer.

There are several physiological reasons why this state of oxytocin-fueled contact feels so good. Higher oxytocin decreases blood pressure and heart rate, lowering anxiety and producing greater calm and relaxation.

Because it's pleasurable, people look forward to almost any sort of physical or emotional touch as a source of more satisfaction. The anticipation of any pleasure activates the release of dopamine, so this gets the brain's reward system churning. As we've seen before, the basic message of the brain in this state is "Keep it coming!"

After friendships are established, the chemical interactions of touchy-feely oxytocin and reward-seeking dopamine, along with the mood-elevating serotonin and endorphins, help us form long-lasting bonds. Losing a good friend can be as painful as losing a lover. Many of the same chemicals and brain circuits are involved in each of these types of relationships.

Women Together

Compared with men, women tend to make friends with other women quite easily. Generally speaking, you can leave two women in a busy doctor's waiting room and by the time they're called for their appointments, they know each other's life story and have traded phone numbers. Much of the cause behind this behavior has to do with women's brains and hormones.

Most women, far more than men, mirror other people and their emotions exceptionally well. Because of estrogen and a greater default level of oxytocin, women feel more in their bodies than men do, from their emotions and physical sensations of pain, pleasure, and everything in between. Women also feel and respond with anguish when faced with another person's pain to a much larger degree than men. If you were to turn on the lights in a movie theater during a particularly violent scene, chances are a large number of the women would be covering their eyes.

Mirror Emotions

A woman sitting with another person immediately begins to mirror that person, matching and simulating his breathing rhythm, muscle tension, and brain circuits. She is able to monitor infinitesimal changes in that person's expression, and search her emotional memory for cues and clues to what he's feeling.

The reason for this difference is that women's brains have many more neuron cells (in both hemispheres) devoted to body sensations and emotional processing. As a result, they're better at anticipating, judging, and integrating emotional reactions, both positive and negative. They read things like someone's pause in speech, the tightness of someone's mouth, or a low, flat vocal tone as essential clues to another person's state of mind and needs. The same clues go right by most men. Knowing the brain science behind these enhanced female powers of perception puts the mystery of "woman's intuition" in a new light.

These enhanced female traits of emotional perception are the vestiges of prehistoric women's need to be nimble enough to discern friends from foes and get the children out of harm's way as fast as possible. If her safety was threatened, she didn't usually stand and fight, as a man of her time (and now) more likely would. She needed the support of other women (and men) to watch and protect their group from external dangers—animal, human, or otherwise. This isn't to say that women always get along with other women. If a woman is competing for a man, or for resources for her children, sometimes she can get quite nasty.

Synchronized Cycles

In addition to women's greater ability to perceive and mirror emotions in others by using visual cues, females have a more perceptive sense of smell than males. It depends again on estrogen, and because women have much more of this hormone, their ability to detect odors is more acute.

One fascinating way in which this heightened sense of smell is thought to work in groups of women is the syncing of their menstrual cycles. This synchronization is believed to happen in a group of women through their inhalation of the menstrual pheromones given off when they perspire. This is apparently the physiological reason behind the much-noted phenomenon of female students living together in dormitories, whose periods occur at the same time of the month as their roommates and dorm mates.

Sex and Friends

Usually, people of the opposite sex begin a relationship knowing from the start whether the connection between them leans more toward a prospective romantic partnership or a friendship. This instant knowledge has traditionally been explained by the presence or lack of "chemistry" between two people. With the science now available to us, it's more correct to say that there's chemistry whether its friendship or infatuation, because we know more about both kinds of chemical interactions.

The chemistry of friendship more closely resembles that of a long-term love relationship. This is the second stage of a romance that has passed through the initial one to two years of intense attraction. It has reached the endorphin- and oxytocin-based phase of comfortable familiarity. Of course, friendship usually doesn't include sex and all its extra chemistry.

How Friends Become Lovers

Once a close platonic friendship has been established between a man and woman, it's unusual (although not impossible) to shift it into a romantic, sexual connection. That's because we become habituated to the different chemistries associated with friendship and romance. Shifting from one chemical circuit to another usually requires an event of some magnitude, whether it's a confession that one of them feels "more than friendship" for the other, or perhaps an extra bottle of wine that removes all inhibitions and lands the two of them in the same bed.

This event then prompts both people to step back and consciously consider a shift in the nature of their relationship. They may opt to stay friends or, if the chemical spark of attraction has ignited in both of them, perhaps they'll try changing the relationship to that of lovers. If this is the way they go, they'll each be instigating a different internal chemistry toward the other person. Will the new chemistry last, or will one or both opt to go back to the tried-and-true circuit of friendship? Or will they decide that it's simply too awkward and end their friendship all together? That is the question.

It's a high-stakes transaction when friends up the ante and add romance to their platonic relationship. With the extra chemical intensity brought into the mix by physical attraction and sexuality, they are launching an inherently more combustible relationship. If there's a romantic break-up, the friendship can be harmed or lost. However, if both parties know and understand the extra stress these chemical fireworks will bring, they can reap the rewards of greater trust and familiarity of the friendship underlying their romance.

Foes

The human brain with the support of our body chemistry is wired to quickly separate those people who are familiar to us, and therefore comfortable, and those who are not. Familiarity depends first and foremost on physical appearance: the facial characteristics, pigment, and size you associate with your family, clan, and culture. Anyone who looks different than you and "your people" is automatically "the other."

Our perceptions of someone and the nature of our relationship with that person determines whether our response will be fight or flight, or calm connection. If our perception is positive, oxytocin will be triggered by something as simple as a smile. With the release of this wonder hormone, anxiety is lower, the person is calmer, and the person's openness increases.

A man's brain is wired for safety and protection. If he perceives another person as a threat, his stress and threat chemicals—norepinephrine, adrenalin, cortisol, and testosterone—will be immediately activated to meet the threat head-on. The reaction might be experienced as a sudden rush and it can make rational thought difficult. Vasopressin will lead him to band with others of his own tribe to fight a larger danger.

It is sometimes dispiriting to see how much of our supposedly enlightened humanity still operates under the heavy influence of its basic testosterone-driven "us versus them" instinct. A majority of the wars fought, let's face it, by men, are based on tribal or ethnic differences. But it's better to understand this aspect of our human nature than to deny it. At least then we can make conscious decisions about whether we wish to work around that instinctual force that leads to more conflict and less cooperation. We have to be careful, though, to not commit what scientists call the "naturalistic fallacy," which is the belief that because something is natural it's good.

Groups

Good social relationships, particularly in groups, keep you healthy. Research shows that people with a shared purpose by way of their participation in a tight-knit club, political party, or religion are healthier psychologically and physically.

These social ties promote the release of oxytocin and endorphins, which are important to good heart and lung function and moods. Close relationships have been shown to assist healing from chronic or acute illnesses. Just one example: the survival rate from breast cancer is higher in women who have a strong circle of support in their lives.

Team Chemicals

In active team sports, players receive the benefits of the chemistry of exercise (endorphins, dopamine) and of bonding (oxytocin) with their teammates. Kinship and group identity are more freely expressed and promoted by physical contact. The high five, group huddles, and celebratory back-slapping that follow a victory on the football field or the basketball court are examples of this natural desire for physical affection and the importance of touching for bonding and near ecstatic touch.

The Chemistry of Competition

In the animal kingdom, there are alpha males and females who call most of the shots. They get the pick of sexual partners and the most sex. They eat more food, take the best spots to sleep, and get to order the others around as they see fit.

In human beings, the same dynamics occur. The primary chemical player behind leadership in men and women is testosterone. The hormone vasopressin, which, like testosterone, is present in higher quantities in men's bodies, is thought to support the formation of brotherly ties among unrelated males with the purpose of fending off a common enemy. It does this by tamping down testosterone, which is responsible for a man's aggressive, competitive tendencies. The right balance of teamwork and aggressive individual performance is essential for team sports. Similarly, these hormones must find the right balance inside each individual player on the field.

Woman vs. Woman for a Man

A woman's tendency to feel threatened by another woman, like a man when confronted by a competitor of his own sex, has ancient roots. A modern woman's fight (not flight) response can still be activated when "her man" becomes the prey of another woman, say evolutionary scientists. They speculate that, on an unconscious, primal level, such competition threatens a woman's source of food and protection.

Maryanne Fisher, author of this book, has examined how women compete with other women for men. In one study, she asked women who were menstruating, and therefore in an infertile phase, to rate the facial attractiveness of other women. She compared their ratings against women who were ovulating and thus most fertile. The argument was that the highly fertile women should be most competitive because this is the time when it's important to find a high-quality mate, so they should provide lower ratings of potential rivals. One way women compete is in terms of their physical attractiveness, so by providing lower ratings, women are derogating potential competitors when it matters most.

Strategies in Female Competition

In another study, Maryanne Fisher found that women (and men) compete for mates in at least four ways. The most prevalent is to simply make themselves look as good as possible relative to any rivals, which is called self-promotion. This is a great strategy because it helps one compete against many rivals at the same time, and allows people to deny that they are competing at all. Imagine a woman is going out for a night on the town with a group of friends. She'll look her best, wear fancy perfume, and try to have the most outgoing personality. If someone accuses her of competing, she can simply say that she was trying to look and feel her best. Nothing wrong with that!

The next most popular strategy is competitor derogation, where someone tries to make a rival look bad. If two men are interested in the same woman, one might tell the woman that his friend is a real womanizer or is very deceptive.

Another strategy is mate manipulation, such as when someone tries to influence a potential mate by guarding them so they have no time for a rival. A final strategy is competitor manipulation. When two women are competing for the same man, one woman might tell the other that the man is gay or that he has a sexually transmitted disease, hoping that her rival will lose interest.

Co-Workers and the Chemistry of Cooperation

Business is about human relationships. Although hugs and backrubs are off limits in most workplaces, the very basic human need for trust is a necessity for pairs and teams of people to reach common objectives, whether that objective is selling soap in a Madison Avenue advertising agency or educating children in a suburban public school. The chemistry of trust is very similar to the chemistry of friendship. The essential ingredient necessary for establishing and maintaining trust is oxytocin.

 TURN-OFF

If you demonstrate through your body language that you're not listening attentively to someone, e.g., avoiding eye contact and leaning away, you'll probably produce a fight-or-flight reaction in that person. Her vasopressin and norepinephrine will take over from the oxytocin and endorphins that promote bonding and connection.

Researchers have done studies in a variety of workplaces that reveal the importance of this bonding chemistry. Even if you don't develop deep friendships with your co-workers, it appears that in order to work together successfully, you and your office mates must exercise the same brain and body circuits that you use with your personal and romantic partners.

Claremont College "neuro-economist" Paul Zak, who has done controlled experiments in workplaces involving oxytocin, calls these relationships "temporary human attachments" that depend on trust. In his experiments, Zak has shown that the exchange of friendly social signals releases their trust-building chemistry. He also found that giving people an injection of oxytocin influences their behavior by making them more generous.

Everyday Encounters

The occasions when you take note of someone walking by or the person you meet on an elevator or at a party can be seen as miniature versions of each of the relationship types covered in this chapter. Someone's appearance, body language, and the presence of incentives for competition or cooperation of the sort you have at work or on a team can spark a chemical reaction that then shapes your response.

Here's a useful fact in love or friendship: a 20 second hug is what is needed to cause the release of oxytocin. However, when in doubt, remember the power of a smile. One experiment showed that the simple act of smiling promotes the release of oxytocin in the one who smiles, as well as in the person being smiled at.

The Least You Need to Know

- Women use their enhanced powers of smell and emotional perception to bond and as a first line of defense with members of their own sex.
- Before changing a friend into a lover, be prepared for the volatility that accompanies the chemistry of attraction and romance.
- Teamwork at play or on the job depends on the chemistry of trust and connection, which can and must be cultivated if yours is to be a winning team.

The Chemistry of Awe: Baby Chemistry

In This Chapter

- The chemicals that prepare new mothers and fathers for parenthood
- What happens when bird and human fathers have too much testosterone and a nest filled with young
- Which senses are most important in mother/child bonding
- Why the chemical imprints formed in early childhood last a lifetime

Take a moment to thank your mother. She is the one who taught you how to trust and bond, and to anticipate the lifelong rewards that come through your attachments to other human beings. The chemistry and emotions that started with Mom then expanded in widening circles to include Dad, sister, brother, aunts, uncles, and grandparents. When you're old enough and find the right partner, the process begins again as you bring your own child into the world. Here science and the miraculous co-exist happily in the same amazing story.

Birthing, Babies, and Bonding

As has been true for many millennia, a woman's biochemistry prepares her brilliantly for giving birth, and then readies her for the feeding and nurturing of a newborn baby. During pregnancy, her brain circuits were rewired, and her senses attuned for the extra demands of caring for a newborn. As a result of her evolutionary instincts and this intense chemical preparation, she will focus nearly all of her attention and energy on this tiny person until his survival is assured. And compared to other animals, this period of motherly attention is unusually long.

Oxytocin and Vasopressin

Throughout the animal kingdom, oxytocin is fundamental to the first bonding that occurs after a baby is born, as it is in humans. Much of what is known about the role of this hormone in creating and maintaining human bonds comes from animal experiments. Female rats and sheep (ewes) given injections of oxytocin will take care of young rats and young lambs they've never seen before.

Vasopressin plays a larger role for men in order for them to make the emotional connections required by new fatherhood. It does this by promoting monogamy and the urge to care for a child.

Mommy and Baby

The "mommy brain" (as neuropsychiatrist Louann Brizendine calls it) is switched on just as the baby makes its way down the birth canal. This happens when the mother's uterine contractions trigger the brain to release a flood of oxytocin and dopamine.

The pain-suppressing effects of these hormones are essential after a woman has experienced anywhere from 6 to 36 hours of labor. Once the baby is born, they create a residue of euphoria as chemical flooding peaks in the first minutes following birth—often coinciding with the first time the newborn is put to his mother's breast for suckling. After giving birth, oxytocin helps the uterus to contract and heal.

It is well known that a mother who has decided to have her baby adopted should not touch the infant, because the act of touching and smelling the baby causes her to release oxytocin. This causes many mothers to reconsider their decision.

During the last month of pregnancy, a mother-to-be starts producing the hormone that prepares her for nurturing and lactation: prolactin. This hormone causes milk to be secreted from the breast. Oxytocin assists by enabling the milk let-down response in a woman's breasts and sensitizing the new mother to her infant's touch. In fact, the handling of a woman's breasts, whether it be by an infant or by a mate, causes oxytocin to be released.

Higher levels of prolactin and oxytocin also cause low sexual desire in a new mother. The presence of prolactin decreases her testosterone and depresses her general sensations and alertness. During nursing, oxytocin surges, bringing pleasure and relaxation to the mother and deepening the mother/infant bond.

SEXY FACT

Some women say they've experienced orgasms while nursing their babies. Between the stimulation of a woman's breasts and nipples, and the flooding of her brain and body with pleasurable oxytocin, it's certainly possible.

Daddy and Baby

The latest studies have shown that expecting and fathering a baby changes a man's brain, too. Right after hearing the news that he's about to be a father, men start to produce cortisol, a stress hormone. Cortisol levels tend to spike around four to six weeks after hearing the news, and then decrease as his mate's pregnancy progresses. Then about three weeks before the baby arrives, his testosterone levels fall by about 30 percent, making him more cooperative, less competitive, and more likely to show his softer side.

Also during the last few weeks of his wife's pregnancy, researchers say that a man's prolactin level rises by 20 percent. It's not clear what effect prolactin has in a man, but it is thought to have an indirect impact on those falling testosterone levels. After his child's birth, his estrogen level, a nurturing influence that is normally very low in a man, increases. The point of these changes is to make fathers more maternal in their behaviors, more than their normally high levels of testosterone will allow. About six weeks after birth, his hormone levels begin to return to normal.

Experiments carried out with several species of monogamous birds found that those male birds with higher testosterone levels tended to be absentee fathers who went off for a polygamous turn while the mother bird tended her nest of hatchlings. In men, higher testosterone has also been shown to increase infidelity and decrease nurturing skills. Fortunately, most male birds and human males are more willing to settle into domesticity during the early days and months of infant care.

What else happens to new human dads? With lower testosterone, their sex drive drops, too. Some researchers believe that pheromones are at work in preparing macho men to become doting dads, at least for the first few weeks. This scenario has men receiving his wife's pregnancy chemicals through his sense of smell, and then becoming more like her.

His higher estrogen, along with lots of skin contact with his baby, triggers oxytocin in a man, which helps to reinforce a father's new-found cuddling and cooing behaviors. Still, fathers interact with infants and toddlers in different ways than mothers. A father is more likely to jiggle or rock babies in a playful, rhythmic fashion, while women use firm or light touching to soothe and contain them. As children grow older, a father tends to take a more rough-and-tumble approach to their physical care, and be more challenging and less sympathetic than a mother. Research shows that both approaches are good and necessary for developing children.

Daddy and Mommy

Preparation is everything when it comes to a new baby! It's especially useful for new parents, who need to appreciate in advance just how much this new member of the family will change their relationship. For starters, because of the new mother's flooding of oxytocin and dopamine as a result of giving birth, and then nursing her baby, a mother is quite literally "in love" with this new tiny person. Sorry, Dad, for the moment you come second.

TURN-OFF

When his wife falls in love with her newborn baby, a father can feel jealous and left out. This is normal, hormonally driven behavior. It's also temporary, but husbands should not be in too much of a rush to return to regular lovemaking; her libido is likely to be lower for up to a year.

Sociologist Arlie Russell Hochschild noticed that having children can create a "time bind," where parents begin to feel very pressured to meet obligations at home but simply don't have the time. Sometimes parents begin to resent each other because of the time demands that are expected to maintain a romantic relationship in addition to looking after children, maintaining a household, engaging in a social life, and being successful at work. She found that although most parents believe that family comes first, parents often enjoyed their work lives more than their home life. Work life is often seen as rewarding, leading to feelings of success and accomplishment, while home life is seen as a source of stress because there is simply too much to do with too little time.

While she's nursing, a new mother will find that her brain stays fuzzy and forgetful, thanks to oxytocin and prolactin in great quantities. Together, this leads a new mom to have "mommy brain" where she's happy but easily distracted and unfocussed. Add in the usual lack of sleep for a good six months after a baby is born, and nothing will feel the same to the new mother or father—because it isn't.

Finally, certain sexual behaviors with her partner can temporarily be dangerous to a new mother, given that her body has just undergone such a radical change. Couples should be sure to get a post-natal checkup before engaging in sexual activity.

The Chemical Co-Dependent Bond

Maternal, nurturing behavior is not strictly a new biological parent's prerogative. Older siblings, adoptive parents, grandparents, caregivers, and others will respond maternally after they experience close daily contact with an infant. Physical cues from the baby about her needs for feeding, a dry diaper, holding, or calming will forge new neurochemical pathways in a caretaker like those in a new mother. These brain changes are then reinforced by an influx of oxytocin from skin-to-skin contact with the baby.

Mommy, Daddy, and Baby

A somewhat different chemical stew featuring oxytocin, dopamine, and endorphins enables a family to maintain and build on the bonds formed around the birth of a new baby. At its best, this chemistry offers parents and children the calm, connection, and attendant pleasures of family life. It can also create a buffer to weather the inevitable storms that come when raising children and growing up.

Smells and Family Love

A mother will learn the unique smell of her baby's skin (along with her poop and spit-up) within the first few days of the baby's life. She will be able to pick her baby out of a crowded nursery with 90 percent accuracy just using her sense of smell.

Similarly, within a week of birth, babies have a sophisticated ability to discern smells. Preeminent pediatrician T. Berry Brazelton discovered in his clinical work with infants that many infants will refuse a bottle of formula if it's given to them by a lactating mother, but will accept it from the father. Brazelton surmised that it was the smell of the mother's breast milk that made the babies say no to what they apparently decided was the inferior menu option: a bottled meal. It also appears that not any breast milk will do. In Brazelton's studies, infants distinguished a breast pad containing their mother's milk 80 percent of the time from other milk-laden breast pads.

Other research suggests that an infant will only form a fixed sense-memory of mother's smell when she is being touched at the same time, thus allowing one sense-memory to reinforce the other. And, one can surmise, preventing the smell of something completely unrelated (pizza cooking in the oven, cleaning fluids) from replacing Mom's unique smell. This process is thought to be a form of *imprinting*, in that it helps Mom recognize the smell of her baby, and helps the infant recognize his or her mother. Sheep show a similar pattern, such that a ewe will lick her lamb within two to four hours after birth, causing the smell of the lamb to imprint on her brain. That way she can recognize her lamb from all the others.

DEFINITION

Imprinting refers to learning that happens during a very specific time period in development. An individual becomes imprinted to a particular stimulus, such as something or someone in their environment. This is one way we learn who our family members are (and not to consider them as mates).

Children and How They Grow

An infant only has eyes, ears, and every other sense for Mommy for the first few weeks of life. Laboratory tests show that newborns can distinguish their mother's face from other female faces after three days. They can also identify their mother's voice. Add to that the newborn's impressive sense of smell and acute response to touch, and it becomes clear that a baby is recording and responding to the parents' cues immediately after birth.

The powerful imprint of infantile bonding first with mother and then father stays with a child through all the stages of her development into young adulthood. At its chemical roots, this ability to bond is a reflection of the oxytocin response formed between mother and child through the mother's earliest touching and cuddling.

Because of oxytocin's dual role in producing positive emotions and regulating the nervous system, its role is pivotal in creating an emotional or attachment style for a child that is either open or avoidant. The lack of nurturing touch early on can form a negative neurochemical pattern. With negative expectations brought to future attachments, a person will react to the increase of oxytocin caused by physical or emotional intimacy with fear, not with an anticipation of pleasure. Think of it as a blocked or otherwise malfunctioning circuit that can result in problems with later romantic relationships where much of the same chemistry is reactivated.

Instead of the warm and fuzzy feelings activated by oxytocin at the beginning of a relationship, stress chemicals are instead triggered. Cortisol, the chemical that keeps us alert and helps us deal with stress, seems to be the main culprit at work here. And while cortisol is also necessary, for example, to help us wake up in the morning when its concentration in the body is highest, its dampening effect on oxytocin is a less positive thing when we wish to be calm and open to human connection.

Fortunately, if this is the case, it's possible to retrain the brain and build up its oxytocin response through psychotherapy. Therapy can help the person re-frame her thinking and change negative expectations into positive ones. In the process, the brain, which is not a static organ but a very elastic, living part of us, will also change.

Importance of Attachment

Raising a child who is emotionally secure because she has learned to form intimate emotional ties is one of the major challenges of parenthood. The best way to do it is for parents to model the behaviors they wish their children to acquire. The family that communicates openly, has stable and clear rules, allows individual differences, and plays together will have a higher likelihood of producing children with these abilities and qualities. The child is said to be "wired" for happiness, a condition she retains for life.

Attachment Chemistry Grows Up

A baby's drive to bond emotionally with parents and then others is considered part of her biologically based affiliative drive, first discussed in Chapter 2. The unconditional love that she first feels from her parents is internalized as an expectation to be loved by others in spite of her imperfections. This is the basis of self-esteem in any child, and it's also the foundation of a young person's sense of guilt. This is the ability to tell right from wrong based on the ability to empathize with other people. Without attachment bonding in infancy, reinforced by strong family ties where true intimacy (honesty, communication, affection) is modeled by parents and encouraged in children, the later adult has a hard time forming relationships.

More Bonding Chemicals, Please

This early training in forming attachments is an especially important foundation for puberty, a time when kids start to turn away from their parents' reassuring hugs and venture out into a less-nurturing bigger world. Internally, things are also changing radically. Boys face the onslaught of aggressive and competitive testosterone. Girls have their first encounter with the first rollercoaster swings of estrogen and progesterone. Both boys and girls suddenly experience their first feelings of romantic love or sexual desire, leaving the dormancy of childhood behind.

At this precarious time, it's important for parents to help teenagers find continuing sources of the calming, connection-promoting hormones oxytocin and endorphins. Activities for teens that provide this important kind of stimulation include team or individual sports, and clubs that encourage physical activity and teamwork.

The Least You Need to Know

- A new mother's chemistry is baby-centered, presenting a challenge to her when she must split her time and focus between work and child, her newborn and other children, or between husband and child.

- If oxytocin-based bonding is not provided sufficiently by mother (or another caregiver) to the baby in the days after childbirth, an avoidant attachment style may be imprinted in the brain, making intimacy more difficult later.

- It's important to help teenagers find new sources of oxytocin and endorphins after they leave the safety and security of a more sheltered family life.

Love Chemistry for Mature Couples

In This Chapter

- The chemistry of hot flashes
- How one stress hormone can cause impotence
- The risks and rewards of male and female hormone-replacement treatments
- The good news waiting for you on the other side of menopause

Many folks over 50 who are enjoying life with a long-term partner believe that of all the stages in the chemistry of love, the best is saved for last. That's if you can imagine parting with the hormonal roller coaster that has been ruling you since adolescence. Unlike every previous stage, the chemical transformations that take place can make older men and women more alike in their temperaments and sexual desires. The result can be the removal of many of the contentious issues that arose in decades past due to different chemistries. On the other hand, the changes that occur at midlife represent the biggest chemical transformations since puberty, especially for women.

Today's brain science is adding shading and texture to the picture that has traditionally been painted of women "after the change." About men, the fact that there actually is a menopause, called "andropause" by some, may be news to you. As you would expect, chemistry rules that change, too.

As always, what you know in advance about your changing brain and body chemistry will save you worries later. The landscape ahead for mature couples is full of opportunities to fulfill aspirations alone and together that you've been putting off. Well, the time is now! Make the most of it.

Women Age, Hormones Change

The average age that a woman reaches menopause is 51 years, although for approximately 15 percent of women, menopause occurs noticeably earlier, around age 45. Thanks to the maturing baby boom, about 150,000 American women enter menopause every month. The estrogen and progesterone that made her a menstruating, childbearing woman are taking their curtain call.

Chemical and Physical Changes

It's unlikely that anyone, male or female, has ever bemoaned the end of PMS. Who would shed tears for monthly cramps, bloating, a short temper, and mood swings? But when her periods come to an end, a woman is greeted by menopause, literally a pause (more like a slow tapering off) of her menses. Although menopause causes unpleasant physical symptoms for 85 percent of women, the good news is that these problems last a much shorter time than the three to four decades a woman typically contends with her monthly menstrual cycles. Every woman is different: 30 percent of menopausal women experience severe symptoms and 15 percent have none or few.

These are some of the common physical effects of menopause:

- *Hot flashes* and flushes (flushed cheeks, chest)
- Night sweats
- Memory lapses
- Depression, anxiety
- Heart palpitations
- Irritability

- Headaches

- Body pains

- Dry, thin skin

- Difficulty falling or staying asleep

- Hair loss

- Cravings for sweets and carbs

- Incontinence

We've come a long way since the days when women were told that the chemical changes of menopause were figments of their aging imaginations.

DEFINITION

What causes a **hot flash?** Although the details of what happens are not entirely clear, we know that decreasing estrogen acts upon the hypo-thalamus, which regulates body temperature. A woman's skin can heat up by seven to eight degrees, with accompanying skin reddening, which can last up to five minutes.

Although menopausal symptoms have long been spoken of, and often joked about at women's expense, there's now science to explain how and why they occur. There is a time immediately before menopause called "perimenopause," the years in which the levels of estrogen and progesterone become more irregular and fertility decreases. This can begin around the age of 35, although most women do not realize they are in perimenopause until their mid-40s.

Interestingly, there is considerable cross-cultural variation in the experience of menopause. Women in Japan rarely experience hot flashes, but instead experience tight shoulders where movement is painfully impaired. We don't know why this is. It may be because a Japanese diet is different, or that the culture of Japan includes an acceptance of elderly women, thus reducing the stress of being old.

Impact of Estrogen Decline

Because estrogen modulates the brain's levels of the neurotransmitters serotonin, norepinephrine, and acetylcholine, its relative absence unbalances these mood- and memory-regulating chemicals, too. Many menopausal women take an SSRI antidepressant to prop up their mood-regulating neurotransmitters.

Estrogen also triggers the brain's release of dopamine, the motivating and pleasure-producing neurotransmitter that a menopausal woman has in smaller quantities.

And there's more. Because of less estrogen in her body, a woman's brain has a different response to glucose, causing energy surges and drops. This chemical change is behind her cravings for sugary and starchy treats.

Finally, without estrogen to trigger oxytocin, the woman in menopause has far less of the calm- and connection-promoting impulses driven by this hormone. This one change has far-reaching physical and psychological impact. Many menopausal wives and mothers lose interest in the caretaking activities that were central to their childbearing, husband-, and household-tending years.

> **POINTER**
>
> Spoken or unspoken messages like "Do your own laundry" or "Make your own dinner" from a menopausal woman to adult children are typical, although sometimes shocking if you were used to having a "super-mom" who always tended to your needs before her own. It may help to know that her changing hormones are at least partly "making" her do it. Then learn to cook and do that laundry!

The fact that many children grow up and move out of their parents' homes around this time in a woman's life usually works in sync with her chemically driven need to put her energies elsewhere.

Supplementing with Hormones

Women have gone from being told that the symptoms of menopause are all in their heads to finding relief through herbal supplements or prescriptions, only to find out that these remedies can cause further health concerns. Women now find themselves in limbo. If you're confused, you're not alone. But rather than doing nothing, or trying something unproven, the answer is to consult with your health provider to find out what's right for you.

HRT

Hormone-replacement therapy (HRT or HT)—taking supplements of estrogen and progestin (a form of progesterone) in pills, patches, vaginal cream, or gels—can reverse many of the troubling symptoms related to a woman's menopausal decline of these two hormones. It's also often referred to as estrogen replacement (ER) if just estrogen is targeted. One popular form of estrogen therapy, at least from the late 1990s to 2002, was Premarine, which is derived from horse (mare) urine.

Unfortunately, after hormone-replacement therapy achieved a high level of use and popularity among perimenopausal, menopausal, and postmenopausal women in the 1990s and early 2000s, an important long-term study by the Women's Health Initiative (WHI), carried out between 1993 and 2005, came along to provide serious cause for concern. The decision to use hormone-replacement therapy became far more complex after WHI found that increased risks exceeded the benefits of HRT; they discovered that women who take estrogen plus progestin were at higher risk for heart disease, blood clots, stroke, and breast cancer.

Summary of WHI findings:

- Use of combined estrogen plus progestin supplements longer than five years nearly doubles subsequent breast cancer risk each year.

- The recent reduction in breast cancer (after the original study was halted in 2003) incidence is primarily related to a decrease in estrogen plus progestin use.

- HRT put women at a lower risk of colon cancer and bone fractures.

This set of findings caused a great deal of confusion, with new guidelines for HRT not yet clear. That means the decision must be made on an individual basis between every midlife woman and her healthcare provider. To make this decision, she must balance her relative health risks against the rewards of using HRT according to her family health history, age, duress of menopausal symptoms, and any other existing medical conditions, to arrive at what, if any, dosages and duration are appropriate to her situation.

Testosterone

During menopause, women continue to naturally produce smaller amounts of testosterone because their adrenal glands continue to function. Many women are able to increase lost sexual desire using prescribed testosterone during menopause. Although some evidence exists that supplementing with testosterone during menopause may increase sexual response, there are health risks and potential side effects associated with testosterone supplements in women.

In particular, one study in the *Archives of Internal Medicine* found that women who used both estrogen and testosterone supplementation during menopause experienced a 17.2 percent increase in breast cancer risk for each year of use.

Other vitamin and synthetic hormone supplements and lifestyle changes have helped some women reduce their menopausal discomforts. Getting regular exercise, eating less sugar and carbs, drinking only moderate amounts of alcohol, and eating more soy products are some of the popular and potentially safer options.

Sex and the Older Female

Fifty percent of women ages 42 to 52 report that they have experienced a decrease in their sex drive. Menopausal women may lose interest in sex, or be harder to arouse, and/or have fewer and less intense orgasms. One cause of lower libido is that, by the time a woman enters menopause (technically 12 months after her last period), she has lost 60 percent of the testosterone she had at age 20.

Fortunately, this is not the end of the story for older women and their sexuality. For many a woman, sex drive reappears with new gusto on the other side of her most severe menopausal symptoms.

Expectations Matter

Studies show that an older woman's mindset about her body, her marriage/relationship, and her age has a sizeable impact on her experience of sex after she enters menopause. Researchers at the New England Research Institute and the University of Massachusetts Medical School have discovered that the key factors influencing which women have problems with menopausal and postmenopausal sex drive and sexual response include individual attitudes toward sexuality and overall health and marital status.

Significantly, they found that estrogen is not related to changes in sexual response in postmenopausal women. In particular, only women who believed that loss of interest in sex was a normal part of the aging process actually saw a decrease in their sexual desire. The researchers also determined that only painful sexual intercourse, and not overall sexual desire, was directly related to decreased estrogen production during menopause.

In summary, the sex-related changes associated with menopause for women include the following:

- Lower sexual desire, attributable to lower testosterone and other nonchemical factors

- Vaginal dryness and pain during intercourse, a direct result of lower estrogen

- Heat sensitivity from hot flashes and flushes, along with insomnia and other physical discomforts connected to menopause can also dampen a woman's sex drive, and sexual response while these symptoms are most severe

Becoming informed about the risks and rewards of different forms of treatment for bothersome menopausal and sexual symptoms is essential. So is an emotional self-assessment. Your attitudes and self-concept may be more of a factor than you may have realized in your sexual identity.

Jaguars on the Prowl

Because "cougar," in the context of women's sexuality, popularly refers to a woman over 40 with a preference for younger men, we've adopted the "jaguar" as an animal totem for her slightly older, still sexy sisters. The concept of "postmenopausal zest" came originally from famed anthropologist Margaret Mead, referring to the second wind many older women experience in their sixties. This zest often manifests as a greater vigor and verve toward life and sexuality once women pass through the initial symptom-plagued stage of menopause. Without the worries of pregnancy and PMS, or the burdens of parenthood, these women wake up and feel sexy again. Inside a marriage, this can be a second honeymoon for a couple with the time and inclination to reshape their relationship and bring back sexual passion that might have waned.

On the other hand, not all marriages survive these chemical changes and emotional challenges. In fact, three quarters of divorces for people after the age of 50 are initiated by women.

For women in their forties through sixties who are hitting the dating scene after divorce or widowhood, an increasing number are reported to have sexual fulfillment in mind with no real desire to remarry. In this media-fueled popular narrative, a cougar or jaguar's prey is younger men who want to enjoy what a sexually experienced older woman can bring to the bedroom.

Men Aging

Some call the chemical changes experienced by men at midlife "menopause lite." Others refer to it as "andropause" (androgen is another word for testosterone). Some in the medical profession reject the notion of male menopause entirely. For the sake of our discussion in this chapter, we'll use the term male menopause as a catch-all for the hormonal and physical changes that commonly occur to the over-50 male. There's no question that a man's chemical balance changes at this stage, just not as much or as fast as a woman's.

Although not as familiar as the signs of female menopause, the chemical, biological, and psychological transformations a man goes through at this stage of life can feel equally large and troublesome to individual men. This is especially true if they happen to coincide with another major change in his life such as a job loss, divorce, or something purely physical such as weight gain or baldness. Then the experience can throw a man so far off his equilibrium that he's said to be experiencing a "midlife crisis," which often starts when a man is in his forties when his testosterone begins to decrease.

These are some of the body and brain changes that are frequently grouped under the heading of male menopause:

- Back pain, sore joints, and stiffness

- Weight gain

- Decreasing muscle mass and fitness

- Fatigue and low energy

- Depression, irritability, bad temper

- Loss of memory and concentration

- Lower motivation and competitive edge

Unlike menopause in women, which represents a well-defined period in which hormone production stops completely, testosterone decline in men is a slower process. The testes, unlike the ovaries, do not run out of the substance it needs to make testosterone. However, subtle changes in the function of the testes may occur as early as 45 to 50 years of age, and more dramatically after the age of 70 in some men. A healthy male may be able to make sperm well into his eighties or longer, which means that men can become fathers at almost any age. The quality of the sperm is lower, though, which means that any children of older men are more likely to have genetically caused disabilities.

Lower Testosterone

Like a woman's diminished supply of estrogen, a man's testosterone level begins to drop in his thirties, sliding downward about 1 percent per year afterwards. By about age 70, the decrease in a man's testosterone level can be as much as 50 percent. Due to lower testosterone, a man's desire for sex will gradually lessen from its peak in his early twenties, but high levels typically continue through his thirties, and then decrease in his forties.

Some doctors refer to this hormonal shift in men as androgen decline in the aging male, or simply low testosterone.

Although not all are related to lower testosterone, the most common sexual problems encountered by men after age 50 include:

- Loss of sex drive
- Erectile dysfunction
- Testicles shrinking and scrotum dropping
- Erection taking longer
- Erection requiring more direct stimulation
- Full erection not being as firm
- Less desire/need for ejaculation and orgasm

To many men, the change to a lower sex drive is not a negative thing. For those who sometimes felt like a slave to high libido, a less-frequent need for sex comes as a welcome relief. It also is much more likely to put over-50 men in the same libido range as their same-age female partners.

Although it's true that impotence (characterized by the inability to develop or maintain an erection, also called erectile dysfunction) increases as an issue and a concern for midlife men, the source of this sexual problem can often be traced to other health issues common to this age range. Among these are: high blood pressure, a prostate condition, diabetes, or heart disease. Other sexual problems can be caused by the medications he's taking for a prior health condition.

Given these factors, when a man encounters media reports on the number of men with impotence problems, he needs to read these carefully. For example, the Massachusetts Male Aging Study reported male impotence at 52 percent of men age 40 to 70. In the fine print, you'll find that this high number puts men with health conditions causing impotence in the same category as men experiencing an impotence problem not attributable to another medical cause. That same study suggests that impotence can be divided into three forms based on how frequently it occurs: minimal, moderate, and complete. They report that 17.2 percent of men experience it minimally, 25.5 moderately, and 9.6 percent completely. They found that age was the main factor, with complete impotence increasing from 5 percent at age 40 to 15 percent at age 70. However, they did not consider the links between heart disease, diabetes, and smoking and impotence, or the potential impact of a man's depression, suppression, or expression of anger.

TURN-OFF

Performance anxiety is a man's psychological reaction to his fear of impotence, or even just not being able to maintain an erection long enough to meet his partner's expectations. This concern has the effect of producing the very thing he dreads: a failed erection. A more relaxed attitude toward naturally occurring changes in sexual performance when he ages is at least a partial antidote.

One very real and common form of erection problem in the aging man is called "psychological impotence." His anxiety about not performing adequately causes an adrenaline reflex, releasing one of the brain's fight-or-flight chemicals as a panic reaction. Too much adrenaline causes blood vessel constriction in the penis as well as elsewhere in the body, such as the capillaries of his skin, causing cold, clammy hands.

Other Chemical Changes

DHEA is the most abundant hormone in the body and parts of it can be transformed into estrogen or testosterone. It also improves cognition, protects the immune system, decreases cholesterol, and serves as an antidepressant. In a man, DHEA drops 3 percent a year after age 25 until age 80 when it is virtually gone. DHEA, which does not show the same decrease in women as they age, is thought to play different roles for each sex. For example, it may increase sex drive in women. DHEA is also thought to be a key factor in male menopause, and (outside the United States) it is used to treat the mental and physical problems of aging as well as male menopause.

Supplementing with Hormones

If testosterone levels are low, testosterone-replacement therapy may help men relieve such symptoms as decreased libido, depression, and fatigue. But as with hormone-replacement therapy in women, testosterone-replacement therapy does have some potential risks and side effects. Replacing testosterone may worsen prostate cancer, for example.

Older and More Alike

The research on mature marriages shows slight variations, but overall it looks like after age 50 the average rate of intercourse for married couples is around once a week. Compare this to 9 times a month for married women at age 30, and 6 times each month for age 40. Another study found that after age 60, the number of couples having weekly intercourse is put at 40 percent of their married age group.

The same Gallup survey showed sexual satisfaction among those couples over 60 at just 20 percent—for both men and women. Beyond the numbers, studies show men to be more sensitive and less forgiving of the vagaries of age in their wives' appearance. Interestingly, the chief complaint among older women concerns their husbands' lack of affection and attention.

As covered in Chapter 2, there are evolutionary drives at work here. Men consider women's physical attractiveness to be very important when selecting a mate. However, whereas women tend to prefer same-aged or slightly older men as they themselves age, men stick with preferring younger women. This means that a 25-year-old man will often find a 20-year-old woman most attractive, which is a 5-year age difference. When he's 50, he'll probably find a 20- to 30-year-old woman most attractive, resulting in a 20- to 30-year age difference.

Although an active fantasy for many older men, this lingering (and evolutionarily bestowed) preference for women of child-bearing age does not appear to dominate the real-life mating behaviors of more than a small minority of males over 60. It mostly is the privilege of society's wealthiest and/or most powerful men, who have the luxury of indulging this fantasy.

Of course, not everything that goes wrong in a marriage has a chemical basis, but these factors are greater than older adults may realize. In part it's because of the sheer volume of hormonal change and rebalancing going on at this time of life. Add to that the possibility of other medical conditions and medications being present in a 60-plus body, and there is even more potential for complex chemical interactions.

When Passion Goes

First, it helps to acknowledge the obvious. As the surveys demonstrate, if you are in your late fifties, sixties, or older and your passion for each other and the relationship is fading or gone, you are not the first and will not be the last couple to face this situation. Long ago, before you married and lived together, it was easy to look your best in each other's presence, to find every conversation interesting, to keep your nasty moods away from each other, to avoid fights over money and children, and to arrange time to be alone without asking anyone's permission.

This, of course, changes after years of close proximity and familiarity, along with the interdependence and demands of family life. One common result is a loss of interest in sex. Emotional difficulties that weren't dealt with earlier in the relationship can drive a deepening wedge between you. If the feelings accompanying a shift away from passion by one or both partners are openly discussed, be they resentment, fear, jealousy, or boredom, there is a good chance that sexuality will re-blossom and you can minimize any damage to your overall relationship.

Compromise about one's sexual needs is like everything else in a successful marriage. There have likely been times when one partner wanted sex and the other wasn't particularly interested. In a successful relationship, giving and receiving pleasure is something to be shared and compromised. At this stage in life, the same dynamics appear.

Sometimes interest in sex returns on its own after one partner resolves an individual medical problem. For example, depression is a diagnosable and treatable mood disorder common to older people and known to put a damper on sexual libido. If you're having trouble working out sexual and relationship problems on your own, many avenues of joint and individual therapy are available to help you address them.

Romance Again?

In many long-term relationships, an extra effort by one or both partners is required to rekindle the spark. A little romantic feeling goes a long way when communication falters and hearts shut down. Said another way, giving and receiving expressions of love and adoration is an effective antidote to the tendency in a long-term relationship to take each other for granted. The best antidote for relationship boredom and to counter some of the downside of aging is to bring back some of the romance you had in the beginning. Let's face it: the oxytocin and endorphins that result from holding hands (or more) perform their magic just as well at 60 as they do at 40 or 15 years old.

Sometimes the prospect of renewing romance is not of interest to both partners. Or they think it isn't. Most men dread Valentine's Day or anniversaries in inverse proportion to the degree that women (of all ages) love to mark these occasions. It's not that deep down, men don't like to be romantic; in fact, they do. Psychologists have established that, contrary to stereotypes, men—more than women—tend to believe in love at first sight and that true love conquers all obstacles. The problem for many a man is his dislike at being told exactly when and how he is supposed to express his adoration for the woman in his life: he must show up with flowers, or jewelry, in lock step with the rest of his gender.

A man who is considering how to reclaim romance in his marriage may prefer to do it in his own way, and then act with authenticity from his own heart. What's in it for the man? With the return of romantic feelings, he potentially gets (back) the woman who used to be mentally, emotionally, and sexually available to him. Now with a little encouragement from him, she is once again ready to receive his love and return it in kind. That's plenty of reward for a small effort.

The Good News

If we take the "glass half-full" perspective on the chemistry of mature relationships, the news is indeed very good. Those couples who still have each other for emotional, intellectual, and sexual companionship into their sixties, seventies, and beyond can look forward to much more commonality in their moods and temperaments than they had in earlier decades. In those years, their vastly different chemistries created many more differences than similarities between them.

This all begins to change as men and women reach the middle of their fifth decade. As testosterone drops, men lose some of the sharpness of their "edge" and become more emotional and often cooperative; in other words, they become more like women. Older women, freed from their monthly estrogen and progesterone cycles, are often less emotional and less changeable in their emotional states than they were before; in other words, they become more like men.

If all goes well, the two of you may find a new middle ground from which you can launch many years of mutual understanding and enjoyment. *C'est la vie.* Such is life, at its best.

The Least You Need to Know

- Male menopause is not universally accepted as a developmental stage in a man's life, but the hormonal changes of the over-50 male and the potential emotional impact of these changes are becoming increasingly understood by the medical profession and by men.

- Hormone-replacement therapy (HRT), specifically involving estrogen, can help mute many of the uncomfortable symptoms of menopause, but because of increased risks associated with its use, women need to discuss their personal risks versus rewards with their personal health provider.

- After women adjust to a lower level of estrogen, and once men get used to having less testosterone, mature couples can find new commonality in their new, more similar chemistry of love.

Putting It All Together

Chapter 19

In This Chapter

- A re-take of the biochemical script behind "love at first sight"
- The top-five lists of love winners and losers
- Testing your love chemistry smarts
- Making love last

Momma can't tell you why you love the way you do. Evolution alone can't explain it. Neither can psychology or neuroscience. But you can still make large strides toward understanding it, if you know the chemistry of the thoughts, emotions, and sexual passions that initially brought the two of you together, and this knowledge can help you love each other over the long term.

While we're at it, how *do* you know that you've just met "the one"? Most people will tell you that they "just knew" within minutes of meeting a sweetheart. As you've gathered from reading this book, this "just knowing," or intuition as some call it, has a scientific basis. Sure, your evolutionary instincts are working hard and your love map is sending out cues, but the glue that binds you and your partner together at the beginning, middle, and end of your relationship is a *chemical connection*. Let's review the essentials and put it all together.

Chemistry as Cupid

A young man and woman are groomed and dressed to please only one person on the planet: the one seated across the table on their first date. From the beginning the sparks are flying. Their conversation is flirty and bubbly. He keeps up his end just fine, although he has to remind himself not to stare at the deep V-neck of her sweater. The sight of her breasts in a push-up bra makes his testosterone spike, adding to the heightened sex drive he already brought to the evening.

Her eyes take in his shoulders, so broad and muscular under his shirt, upping her testosterone, too. Naturally stimulating norepinephrine floods her brain as she focuses all her attention on his face, noticing the symmetry of his features, his firm jaw, and sparkling blue eyes.

Her admiring smile reminds him of the way his mother used to look at him approvingly as a young boy whenever he did something to her liking. This memory produces the pleasurable release of dopamine in his brain, making him anticipate more pleasure as the evening goes on. He lowers his chin and levels a seductive, penetrating look at her.

Her response, spurred by an evolutionary desire to find the right male to produce her future offspring, is thrillingly receptive, enhanced by the release of estrogen and oxytocin in her bloodstream. She signals her mutual interest by reaching across the table and touching his forearm lightly with her fingers, letting her hand rest there.

His oxytocin shoots up, followed by more testosterone and norepinephrine. For these two romantically charged people, this is the moment sealed in their brains, marking when it all began.

His and her PEA are flashing inside their brains with a message: "This just might be 'the One'!" And so it begins … but does it last?

The Embers of Lasting Love

The flames have subsided but the embers of a long-term relationship can still make you plenty warm. You have worked hard to keep your relationship intimate, lively, open, and trustworthy. The chemical concoction that helps you do all that and gives you plenty of rewards in the process is made up of endorphins, oxytocin, serotonin, and your sex hormones estrogen and testosterone.

POINTER

Use what you know about the chemistry of love to keep things new! Remember that PEA and norepinephrine can be activated by anything or anyplace new, scary, exotic, or exciting. And once these agents of "fight or flight" are reawakened, so, too, are your sexual pleasure circuits. That's why sex on vacations can be so much better than it is hanging around the house.

But that doesn't mean the natural stimulants that got things going in the beginning aren't available to you now. By trying new things alone and together, you re-excite your norepinephrine and PEA, and get the dopamine-driven reward system of your brain expecting new and ever-better pleasures. Plus, you get to experience the new with someone you love and trust. It's the best of both worlds!

Top Love Winners

In Chapter 13, we scoured the globe and human history for the best tastes, sights, and ideas to help get the chemistry of love going and keep it on track. These are the things that can capture a heart or keep it. Here are the top five love winners:

- Anything that gets the oxytocin going: touch, smiles, kisses, compliments, brushing fingers—you get the picture

- Moderate amounts of exercise, especially for women experiencing libido or orgasm problems

- Chocolate, in your mouth or in your mind—after centuries of hype, it's the placebo effect on top of a tiny bit of PEA from the cocoa plant

- Good parent/child attachment in your earliest years, getting your chemistry off on the right foot

- The drive to reproduce … the best silent partner for any pair of lovers

There are plenty of other enhancers of your love chemistry to be found in every chapter.

Top Love Losers

In Chapter 14, we warned you about most of these dangerous dampeners of love or libido. They can do their damage at any point in a relationship. So mind these love losers now so you don't have to work harder later:

- Alcohol—far and away the most deceptive of love losers; at first relaxing you but then robbing you of your ability to perform sexually or even feel very much

- Too little food

- Too much food, especially fats, red meat, and dairy

- Hardcore, visual pornography for women

- Speed, including Ecstasy, which causes 40 percent of men to lose erections

If there's a caution, it's that whatever feels "too good, too fast" will probably screw up your sexual health.

A Love Chemistry Quiz

Here's a quick test to see if you've been paying attention thus far. Pick the right answer from the multiple choice or true/false answers listed. The correct answers appear on pages 218–219.

1. The hormone known as the "molecule of monogamy" for its calming impact on male libido is

   a. Vasopressin
   b. Prolactin
   c. Testosterone
   d. DHEA

2. The new chemical added to a relationship after it passes the two-year mark, which accounts for all the warm, fuzzy feelings of familiarity, is

   a. Cortisol
   b. Endorphins
   c. Oxytocin
   d. Estrogen

3. The reward circuit of the brain is activated by all of these human activities or experiences except one:

   a. Hunger
   b. Burning a finger
   c. Sex
   d. Forming social bonds

4. The time marker fMRI researchers correlated most often with the cooling of lust in a new relationship is

   a. One month
   b. One week
   c. Two years
   d. Seven months

5. True or false: 99 percent of married women don't cheat on their husbands

   a. True
   b. False

6. The hormone that makes a woman glow and a man fall asleep post-orgasm is:

   a. Testosterone
   b. Prolactin
   c. Oxytocin
   d. PEA

7. Which person, place, or thing does not go on your love map?

   a. Mom's lipstick color
   b. Dad's cologne
   c. High school sweetheart
   d. Desk at work

8. Pheromones are detected by which human sense?

   a. Smell
   b. Touch
   c. Sight
   d. Taste

9. The human fight-or-flight impulse is most closely associated with which neurotransmitter?

   a. PEA
   b. Dopamine
   c. Norepinephrine
   d. Oxytocin

10. True or false: a woman can become sexually aroused without feeling sexual desire?

    a. True
    b. False

Correct Answers to Chemistry Quiz

1. a

2. b

3. b

4. d

5. b

6. c

7. d

8. a

9. c

10. a

Keeping It All Together

From evolution to what you ate for dinner, everything you do, think, feel, and consume through your five senses, as well as what you remember personally—all of it comes into play. Those are a lot of forces at work. The very best news this book can impart is that each part of the whole, meaning you, including your brain, your feelings, and every cell in your body, is elastic and fluid. You can *always* change things for the better. It's the wonder of chemistry and the miracle of life.

The Least You Need to Know

- Seven hormones and four neurotransmitters are the principle players in your love chemistry.
- The differences between men's brains and women's brains, and the effects of male and female hormones, show up in virtually every aspect of human love and sex.
- The chemical relationship patterns you begin in infancy and have hard-wired in adolescence remain with you throughout your life.
- Men and women are acting on the same evolutionary instinct to reproduce with the most "ideal" member of the opposite sex that each can find.
- This sexual-selection instinct, rooted in the lower or reptilian brain, can lead both sexes to stray outside of marriage.
- The higher brain, meaning the thought, executive functions, and judgment processes of the frontal cortex, are the counterbalance to those chemically supported instincts.

- A knowledge of how the chemistry of lust can hijack the brain's reward system can help put on the brakes and allow better judgment to rule.

- In nature's brilliant plan, the same chemistry that brings you and your sweetheart together in love also welcomes the children you create together as a result.

Glossary

altruism Helping others without direct benefit to oneself.

amygdala Part of the brain that is considered the seat of emotions.

anthropology The study of human evolution (physical anthropology) and human cultures (cultural anthropology).

attachment research The study of how relationships shape mental processes.

clitoris A bundle of nerve-endings located on the vulva that has the sole function of giving sexual pleasure and orgasm to a woman.

cortisol A stress hormone secreted in times of stress to protect the body. Levels of cortisol rise in times of romantic infatuation.

desire Refers to a strong interest in sex and the first stage of female arousal.

DHEA A steroid hormone manufactured mainly in the adrenals but also by the ovaries, testicles, and the brain. It can transform into almost any other hormone.

dopamine A motivating neurotransmitter that's key to the brain's reward system.

egg The female reproductive cell also known as the ovum, which becomes fertile when united with a male sperm.

ejaculation The expulsion of semen from the penis.

epinephrine Adrenaline; a hormone produced by the adrenal glands, it raises blood pressure and increases heart rate and makes breathing faster to prepare for danger or stress.

erection Natural enlargement of the penis when blood flow to the man's pelvic region causes it to become engorged.

estrogen Hormone that regulates secondary sexual characteristics in women and regulates the female menstrual cycle.

hippocampus Part of the brain responsible for short-term memory.

hormones Substances that regulate and control behavior and functions. Not all hormones are directly involved in sexual function, but many are.

hot flash The sensation of sudden warmth in a woman's body related to menopause.

hypothalamus Part of the brain that regulates involuntary systems including temperature, sex, and hunger drives.

impotence A man's inability to achieve or maintain an erection of sufficient firmness for penetration during intercourse.

infatuation May be the first stage of falling in love, characterized by lustful feelings generated by specific hormones and neurochemicals.

inhibited sexual desire When a person feels no desire or a diminished desire to have sex.

labia (majora and minora) External female sex organs that extend from the clitoris to the perineum and enclose the vaginal and urethral openings. Sometimes referred to as the vaginal "lips."

libido Another term for sexual desire.

masturbation Self-stimulation of one's own genitals for sexual pleasures. Can also involve touching other body parts, including breasts, buttocks, anus.

menstrual cycle The hormonally controlled monthly cycle of ovulation, egg development, and sloughing off of the uterine lining that causes blood and tissue to be expelled from the uterus through the vagina.

menstruation The discharge of blood and tissue from the lining of the uterus during a woman's menstrual periods.

natural selection Changes in the gene pool of a species due to differences in the ability of individuals to survive and reproduce.

Neanderthal A species of hominid that flourished in Europe and western Asia from about 300,000 years ago until 50,000 years ago.

nipples The tips of the breasts in men and women that contain erectile tissue and may provide sexual pleasure when stimulated. In women they are connected to milk ducts used to nurse a child during lactation.

neuroscience The study of how the brain gives rise to mental processes.

norepinephrine Central to the brain's emergency response, activating the fight-or-flight system in extreme situations, it puts the body on alert.

orgasm Sexual climax, marked by blood flow to the genitals, involuntary rhythmic contractions of the pelvic muscles, and erotic pleasure.

ovaries The two almond-size glands in the female reproductive system that produce eggs during the monthly cycles and hormones that are involved in sexual responses and the development of secondary sexual characteristics.

oxytocin A hormone important to maternal behavior. It also bonds lovers to each other and parents to children. It reduces anxiety, allowing for relaxation, growth, and healing.

penis The male reproductive sex organ, made up of the shaft, which is the body of the penis, and the head, which is also called the glans.

phallic Relating to or resembling a penis.

phenylethylamine (PEA) A natural form of amphetamine stimulated in the brain during sexual arousal and infatuation causing giddiness and excitement. It spikes at orgasm and ovulation.

plateau The third stage of the sexual response cycle in which the excitement maintains a high level prior to climaxing to the orgasm stage.

premature ejaculation   Ejaculation before the man wants it to occur. It could mean he ejaculates only seconds after the penis enters the vagina, or before penetration.

premenstrual syndrome (PMS)   Disturbances that may occur in women three to seven days prior to their menstrual period. Marked often by moodiness, irritability, bloating, headaches, cramps, and depression. Can be treated to reduce symptoms.

progesterone   An important female hormone, one function of which is to build up the uterine lining to prepare for pregnancy.

progestin   A synthetic progesterone-type hormone used in hormone-replacement therapy and birth control medications.

prolactin   A hormone that stimulates maternal behavior, especially in nursing mothers.

prostate gland   The walnut-size gland that is located below the bladder in a man. It produces the majority of the fluid that combines with sperm and other secretions to make up semen.

scrotum   The pouch of skin that hangs below the penis and contains the male testes.

semen   Fluid containing sperm and seminal and prostatic fluids that is expelled from the penis during ejaculation.

serotonin   A neurotransmitter that is a natural antidepressant and mood elevator.

sexologist   A sexual scientist.

sexual response   The stages of physical and psychological changes that men and women go through in relation to sexual stimulation. These are desire, arousal, plateau, orgasm, and resolution.

sexuality   All aspects of one's personality and behaviors that are affected by one's being male or female.

sperm   The male reproductive cell that is contained in sperm, released through ejaculation, and may be united with a woman's egg to cause fertilization.

testicles (testes) The two small oval glands in the scrotum that produce sperm and male hormones.

testosterone The most influential male hormone, produced in the testicles.

uterus An internal organ of the female reproductive system, also known as the womb.

vasocongestion A physical result of sexual arousal in men and women. In women, vasocongestion involves swelling and reddening of the inner vaginal lips. Breasts may also swell. In men, it is marked by engorgement of blood in the penis that leads to erection.

vasopressin A peptide hormone secreted by the brain that enhances memory, cognition, and alertness. It facilitates assertive/aggressive behavior and discourages emotional and sexual extremes. It increases arousal and returns to normal prior to ejaculation.

Viagra A medication that is used to treat erectile dysfunction in some men.

vulva The term that refers to all of the external female sexual structures: the vaginal openings, the labia, the clitoris, and urethral openings.

Resources

These organizations, hotlines, books, and websites are useful tools to help you learn more about the biology and chemistry of love and life and related subjects. You'll find resources on sexuality, aging, marriage and family therapy, parenthood, drug and alcohol abuse, and child development.

Organizations

American Association of Marriage and Family Therapists
703-838-9808
www.aamft.org

American Association of Sex Educators, Counselors, and Therapists
804-644-3288
www.aasect.org

Sexuality Education and Information Council of the United States
212-819-9770
www.siecus.org

Planned Parenthood
1-800-230-PLAN
www.plannedparenthood.org

American Society for Reproductive Medicine
205-978-5000
www.asrm.com

Drug and Alcohol Abuse Referral Hotline
1-800-821-4537
www.samhsa.gov

American Association of Retired Persons (AARP)
1-800-424-3410
www.aarp.com

Women's Health Initiative (WHI) website offers updates and new data from the study including HRT findings.
www.whi.org

Books

Amen, Daniel G. *The Brain in Love*. New York: Three Rivers Press, 2007.

Brizendine, Louann. *The Female Brain*. New York: Broadway Books, 2006.

Buss, David M. *The Evolution of Desire*. New York: Basic Books, 1994.

Cassell, Carol. *Put Passion First: Why Sexual Chemistry Is the Key to Finding and Keeping Lasting Love*. New York: McGraw Hill, 2008.

Crenshaw, Theresa L. *The Alchemy of Love and Lust*. New York: Pocket Books, 1996.

Fisher, Helen. *Why We Love: The Nature and Chemistry of Romantic Love*. New York: Henry Holt and Company, 2004.

Fisher, Helen. *Anatomy of Love: A Natural History of Mating, Marriage, and Why We Stray*. New York: Random House, 1992.

Greene Baldino, Rachel, and Ford, Judy. *The Complete Idiot's Guide to Enhancing Sexual Desire*. Indianapolis: Alpha Books, 2007.

Kuchinskas, Susan. *The Chemistry of Connection*. Oakland, CA: New Harbinger Publications, 2009.

Locker, Sari. *The Complete Idiot's Guide to Amazing Sex*. Indianapolis: Alpha Books, 2005.

Miller, Geoffrey. *The Mating Mind: How Sexual Choice Shaped the Evolution of Human Nature*. New York: Anchor Books, 2000.

Pease, Allan and Barbara. *Why Men Want Sex and Women Need Love*. New York: Broadway Books, 2009.

Pert, Candace B. *Molecules of Emotion, The Science Behind Mind-Body Medicine*. New York: Simon & Schuster, 1997.

Ridley, Matt. *The Red Queen, Sex and the Evolution of Human Nature*. New York: MacMillan Publishing Co, 1993.

Index